Real Estate Insight: Creating Wealth Through Real Estate Investing

Joseph M. Maas

CFA, CFP®, CLU®, CHFC®, MSFS,
CCIM™, CVA, CM&AA, ABAR

First Edition

Merrell

Published by Merrell Marketing, LLC
13231 SE 36th Street, Suite 215
Bellevue, WA 98006

info@merrellmarketing.com

First Edition

Printed in the United States of America.

Library of Congress Cataloging-in-Publications Data

Maas, Joe

CREATING WEALTH THROUGH REAL ESTATE INVESTING / Joe Maas – 1st ed.

    p.   cm
    Includes index.

ISBN: 978-1-7351658-0-6

"Real estate cannot be lost or stolen, nor can it be carried away. Purchased with common sense, paid for in full, and managed with reasonable care it is about the safest investment in the world."

Franklin D Roosevelt
(January 30, 1882 — April 12, 1945)
Elected U.S. President Four Times

Disclaimer

This book is presented solely for educational purposes and is not intended to represent or be used as an exhaustive financial resource. The information contained in this book is made available for illustrative purposes, explaining only the basics of real estate investing.

The author and Merrell Marketing, LLC, emphasize this material is not offered as financial, legal, accounting, or other professional services' advice. It is highly recommended you seek the services of a competent professional before making any decisions regarding your business or personal finances.

Best efforts have underscored the writing of this book, but the author and publisher make no representations or warranties of any kind and assume no liabilities of any kind with respect to the accuracy or completeness of the contents, and specifically disclaim any implied warranties of use for any particular purpose.

Neither the author nor Merrell Publishing Company, LLC, shall be held liable or responsible to any person or entity with respect to any loss or incidental or consequential damages caused, or alleged to have been caused, directly or indirectly, by the information contained in this book, or disruption caused by errors or omissions, whether such errors or omissions result from negligence, accident, or any other cause.

The case studies with their characters and references are fictional, and any likeness to actual persons, either living or dead, is completely coincidental. Any case studies represented in this book were created to show only the highlights of real estate investing

The reader is advised to consult with a professional financial advisor who has experience establishing real estate plans, and experience advising investors with making choices relevant to their individual financial situation.

Dedication

This book is dedicated to my Lord and Savior, Jesus Christ, my loving wife, Molly, my precious princess, Madison, my amazing son, Andrew, my Church, my mother, Anne Maas, and in loving memory of my father, Henry Maas.

Acknowledgments

We wish to personally thank the following people for their help with creating this book:

Our editor, Dr. Daniel Levine; your expertise, enthusiasm and dedication were invaluable to the success of this book.

The Synergy office staff for your hard work, insightful advice and helpful commentary.

Lindsay Lush for always providing excellent design direction.

Synergy's valued clients, who inspire us to keep moving forward and provide meaning to our work.

About the Author

Joseph M. Maas

Joe Maas is the Chief Investment Officer and lead portfolio manager for Synergy Asset Management LLC (SAM). A highly trained financial analyst, Joe is responsible for analyzing current and potential investments for the firm through deep fundamental analysis, researching industry trends, speaking to industry experts and through a thorough understanding and application of quantitative methods and technical analysis. Mr. Maas is very unique because he is certified in so many areas of expertise. He has earned certificates from nine prestigious organizations, and with over two decades of financial industry experience, his core specialty is providing comprehensive investment management services for individual investors, business owners, and financial advisors.

Mr. Maas holds a variety of world-renowned professional designations; he is a CFA (Chartered Financial Analyst) Charterholder, which is the world's most respected investment professional's achievement. In addition to being a CFA Charterholder, Mr. Maas is a certified valuation analyst (CVA) and is accredited in business appraisal review (ABAR). Mr. Maas' professional capability also includes being a certified merger and acquisition advisor (CM&AA) trained and experienced in buying and selling middle-market companies with revenues from $5 million to $500 million.

Mr. Maas earned his reputation as a Certified Financial Planner™ (CFP®), having fulfilled the requirements of the Certified Financial Planner Board of Standards, and is also a chartered financial consultant (ChFC) qualified to provide comprehensive advanced financial planning.

Adding to Mr. Maas' many skills are his specialties in life insurance and estate planning as a chartered life underwriter (CLU®) and being a certified commercial investment member (CCIM™) with expertise in commercial and investment real estate. In 2000, Mr. Maas earned his Master of Science in Financial Services (MSFS) from The American College.

This Book is for You

Residential Real Estate Investor

For those of you who are intrigued by real estate as an investment, the process of buying and selling a home and the impact it could have on your financial well being.

Commercial Investor

For the commercial real estate investor who understand real estate is part of a larger financial landscape and wants to learn more about the role it plays.

The Insight Series from Merrell Marketing

Available Now:

- Exit Insight: Getting to "Sold!"
- 401(k) Insight: Getting to "Retired!"

New Books Coming Soon!

- Investment Insight: Getting to "Diversified!"
- Startup Insight: Getting to "Funded!"

Contents

Forward

I have known Joe Maas for a number of years on both a professional, and more recently personal level. I am proud to call him a friend. Joe is the epitome of a family man, with a lovely wife and two small children. I met Joe a number of years ago, at a conference where we both were presenting. Upon my first encounter with Joe I was impressed that he has authored a number of financial books and was flattered when he asked me to write the forward for this latest book.

Being in the alternative investment space for over 25 years, it is refreshing to meet someone that is as passionate about alternatives as myself. I currently am the head of alternatives at Direxion, which is a $17B, ETF and mutual fund investment firm. During my career, I have discussed alternative investments within numerous major financial publications and television business outlets. Personally, I consider real estate an alternative strategy that can help diversify an overall investment portfolio. Historically, real estate has shown the ability to help generate an additional source of return within a portfolio, while providing an investment strategy that has the ability to behave differently than equities or bonds.

Over the years, Joe has always been an advocate of alternative investments, and championing them as tools to utilize within a client's portfolio. I have found that there are very few RIAs that are as well rounded as Joe, with the investment acumen to offer real estate options for clients. This book provides some valuable insight on the different investment options and execution of real estate investing. Alternative strategies that tend to be less liquid and involve longer holding periods like real estate, tend to be geared towards high net worth individuals and institutional type of clients.

After reading Joe's book on a guide to investing in real estate, I was really impressed by how this can be a useful resource ranging within the broad spectrum of the investment community, from a novice to a sophisticated investor. The book not only covers the ABCs of real estate investing, but at the same time drills down to those granular details that are often necessary to succeed in the real estate market.

With any investment strategy, it is important to have a plan in place that includes items such as risk tolerance and time horizons. Joe is a very detailed individual with an affinity for numbers. His discipline and structured approach is evident by establishing a blueprint for each client through a personalized investment policy statement that sets the stage to determine if real estate is an appropriate investment option, and if so, what type of real estate is a fit. Joe tackles the question of whether a real estate investment is primarily for income or capital appreciation. This plays a role in the overall determination of what the proper real estate holdings are for a given individual.

An investor's situation can change over time, and Joe's strategy for each client is fluid, as the clients' needs are always being evaluated throughout the process. In the case of real estate, it is vital to have someone who can guide you through the various stages, from soup to nuts. It is rare to find someone with the combination of both investment expertise (CFA Charterholder) along with real estate experience (CCIM). Additionally, having the designation of Registered Investment Advisor (RIA) gives Joe a transparent fiduciary responsibility to his clients. Moreover, Joe is also a Certified Financial Planner (CFP).

There were numerous sections within the book that were especially noteworthy. One of those involved 1031 exchanges, and the nuances associated with it. Whether it was discussing the eligibility for qualifying as a 1031 exchange, the potential tax advantages, or determining if an exchange was viable for your specific scenario, these were all extremely informative. The chapter covering real estate through estate planning is a must read for anyone considering passing on real estate to loved ones. The book also lays out the distinctions between commercial vs residential property and provides an in-depth analysis on the pros and cons of both. Whether someone is "buying" or "selling", this book provides the reader a framework from start to finish. The valuation process is a critical component when buying or selling a property, and Joe's knowledge base of both real estate and finance gives him a competitive edge that very few other advisors possess.

I recommend this book to anyone who has a thirst for knowledge when it comes to investing in real estate, as it has something for everyone, from the first time homebuyer to seasoned investment property owners.

Edward Egilinsky — Managing Director, Direxion

Introduction

"Ninety percent of all millionaires become so through owning real estate. More money has been made in real estate than in all industrial investments combined. The wise young man or wage earner of today invests his money in real estate."

Andrew Carnegie — Scottish businessman and philanthropist

Congratulations. You are ready to buy or sell a new home or perhaps an investment property. You've put together your wish list of features and where you would like to look, but have you taken a hard look at the financial consequences of buying a property and what makes the most sense for your financial future including how taxes may affect your transaction? A residential property is much more than a place to live. It is probably the biggest financial decision you will make. The commitments you make in purchasing a property will influence your lifestyle and your future options. Fall in love with the wrong house and you can lose more than just your down payment. In this book I will introduce you to a new approach to buying and selling real estate; an integrated fiduciary approach that looks at its impact on your overall financial situation, goals and your real estate needs.

A BETTER APPROACH TO INVESTING IN REAL ESTATE

Are you making one of the biggest financial decisions of your life without good advice?

For most individuals, their home is their only real estate investment and may be one of the most profitable investments they ever make. But a home is just the start to opportunities in real estate investing. In this book, I introduce you to opportunities for investing in real estate, the ways you might choose to structure such an investment and some of the benefits and risks of real estate investing.

Real estate has long been a core portfolio holding for wealthy investors and a path to wealth for many individual investors. In addition to the ability to leverage the purchase of real estate and increase the impact of appreciation on your investment, real estate can offer on-going income and favorable risk-return tradeoffs that result from its uniqueness and the relatively inefficient markets in which real estate trades.

As with all investments, the risk of loss as well as the potential for profit exists. A successful real estate investment depends not just on the property, but also how it fits your financial situation and goals. My team and I have built and refined an institutional fiduciary process that offers investors what we very much believe is a better approach to buying and selling real estate — An integrated approach that looks at its impact on your overall financial situation and goals and current opportunities in the real estate market. This approach is overseen by our team of Certified Financial Planners (CFP), Chartered Financial Analyst (CFA Charterholder), investment advisory representatives, engineers, and our professional real estate agents and Certified Commercial Investment Member (CCIM).

RETHINKING THE REAL ESTATE INVESTMENT PROCESS

Many real estate investors are accidental investors. At one point they may have purchased a home that they later decided to turn into a rental property to generate monthly income or wanted to realize additional appreciation on the property in a high demand environment. The decision could also have resulted from a fall in real estate values when the owners were unable to recover the equity they had invested and opted to wait to sell in a more favorable market.

While accidental investing has worked for many, there is a wide range of real estate investment opportunities available to consider from sole ownership of a property to real estate investment trusts and partnerships, from multi-family residential to office buildings and shopping centers. The catch is to make certain the transaction is in your best interest and fits your financial goals.

The fiduciary process I deploy is unique in that it is positioned to offer both real estate and investment advice to help investors make sound real estate investment buying and selling decisions in the best interests of their long-term financial future.

In the following pages, I will take a holistic approach to real estate; an approach that looks at its impact on your financial future as well as your desire to have an investment property that fits your lifestyle.

About the Book

Land has been a source of wealth since the first men laid out their boundaries and said, "Mine." The value of land is both that of a prized possession — a home, a place where one can shut the door on the world or welcome it in — and as an asset that produces value in the form of crops, livestock, minerals, rental income or use fees.

Real estate has one very big advantage over other assets. It's tangible. At the end of the day, there is a physical property. As with any investment, there is the opportunity for loss as well as profit. Facilities can become obsolete. Locations can lose value due to circumstances beyond the owner's control. Real estate can be mismanaged. Performance can be overstated. But as long as the land remains, tangible value remains. Even in the worst real estate declines, losses in value are hard pushed to approach the bursting of the tech bubble in 2000-2002 when the Nasdaq index lost 70% of its value and the S&P 500 index fell nearly 50%.

In the following pages, we explore the ownership and creation of wealth from developed land — residential, commercial or industrial properties. While farms, ranches, mineral properties, recreational properties and other land categories have wealth-creation potential, they generally require more specialized knowledge and the ability to work the properties.

In particular, we are looking at properties that increase in value over time from appreciation and also have the ability to generate steady cash flow through rental income. These are properties that a wide range of investors with different knowledge and physical abilities can purchase and potentially profit from in a number of different ownership forms.

As with any investments, real estate is not risk free. Regardless of the ownership form, real estate investments are considered highly speculative and involve a high degree of risk. The inherent risks to real estate investing include but are not limited to:

- the destruction of the property through an uninsured event, such as earthquake, flood or war
- the absence of guaranteed income or cash distributions
- lack of liquidity
- measurable and immeasurable risks of owning, managing, operating and leasing properties
- possible conflicts of interests with managers and affiliated persons or entities
- the risks associated with leverage
- tax risks, including changes in tax law
- declining markets and challenging economic conditions
- as well as the risks associated with executing a §1031 exchange (explained in subsequent chapters) including but not limited to:
  — disallow ability of a §1031 exchange
  — fees to execute an exchange
  — known or unknown regulatory challenges

Because partial ownership of real estate may require the purchaser to be an accredited investor, there must be a reasonable expectation by the investor that qualification will continue into the future. Accredited investors are required to have a net worth of $1,000,000 or more, not including their primary residence and/or have an income over the last 2 years of $200,000 for an individual or $300,000 for a couple. Businesses, trusts and other entities may also qualify as accredited.

Creating Wealth Through Real Estate Investing

Chapter 1:
Creating Wealth Through Real Estate

"Real estate investing, even on a very small scale, remains a tried and true means of building an individual's cash flow and wealth."

Robert Kiyosaki — author of the
#1 personal finance book of all time

Throughout history, the ownership of property has been a sign of wealth and a path to greater riches. But successful real estate investing doesn't come without risk. This book is written to help increase your probability of making successful investments and to help you understand some of the many paths and forms of real estate ownership.

Historical Performance

When one evaluates investment options, the first question is typically price appreciation. What has been the asset class' increase in value been over time? Over longer periods of time, the S&P 500 has produced average annual returns of 9-10%. Real estate, on the other hand, has tended to slightly outpace inflation. The average value of new residential properties has increased 5.5% on an annualized basis since 1950. When that number is adjusted for the increased size of new homes (in 1950, a new home averaged 980 square feet*), returns hover closer to 1.6%.

---

* National Association of Home Builders data reported in McMansion: A Closer Look At The Big House Trend by Lisa Smith, updated June 25, 2019 - Investopedia https://www.investopedia.com/articles/pf/07/mcmansion.asp

One of the most accurate measures of changes in the residential market is the S&P 500 Case Shiller Home Price Index which tracks repeat sales of the same home. The national index is a composite of single-family home price indices for the nine U.S. Census divisions. The index shows the price of existing homes increasing by slightly under 4% annually for the ten years ending December 2019.

S&P 500 CoreLogic Case-Shiller
U.S. National Home Price NSA Index

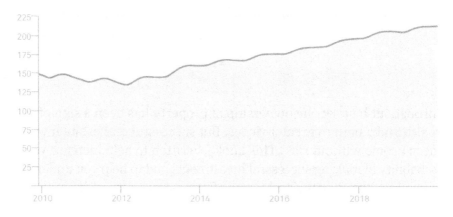

As of **Dec 2019**
Published **Feb 25, 2020**

Source: https://www.spindices.com/indices/indicators/sp-corelogic-case-shiller-us-national-home-price-nsa-index

Commercial properties outpaced housing gains over the same period on a national basis, but only slightly, with apartment properties outperforming core commercial, retail, industrial and office properties.

Annualized S&P 500 Index return for the same period was slightly under 11%.

It is also important to note the real estate returns vary widely based on geographic region and can be adversely impacted by demographics, economic conditions, interest rates, and government policies. Like other investment classes, real estate is subject to cyclical market swings and to falling prices. The unprecedented increase in house prices starting in 1997 peaked in 2006 and the "great" housing bubble burst with home prices falling more than 34% in markets throughout the U.S. While many markets recovered to their earlier highs, real estate prices remain depressed in areas throughout the U.S.

Does this mean real estate is a less desirable investment? Not at all.

Advantages of Real Estate Investing

Real estate has three very significant advantages over other asset classes.

- Leverage
- Income generation
- Tax advantages

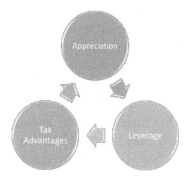

Leverage

Real estate is one of the very few investments where lenders will gladly loan 80% or more of the purchase price for extended time periods and at better interest rates than are available on virtually any other asset.

When it comes to buying a personal residence, lenders typically require 20% as a down payment to finance the remaining 80% of the purchase price. With VA and FHA financing, down payments can be even lower (although you will have to pay mortgage insurance if you have less than 20% of the purchase price in equity). Residential real estate financing features some of the lowest interest rates available because the loan is secured with a mortgage against the homeowners' property.

Minimum down payments of 20-25% of the purchase price are commonly required to finance commercial or investment properties and lenders tend to charge a slightly higher interest rate.

The benefit of leverage is that small returns can be greatly amplified. Let's assume an investor purchases a townhouse for $250,000 with a 20% down payment.

Purchase price: $250,000
20% Down Payment: $50,000
Mortgage: $200,000

If the property appreciates 4.75% annually over the next four years, the homeowner gains $50,000+ in equity, a 100% cumulative gain on the down payment of $50,000. Naturally, it's not that simple. You would also have to consider any costs incurred in purchasing the property, and payments for interest, principal, taxes, insurance and utilities over the investment period. There's also the possibility that the investor will need to make improvements to the home during the years the property is held, adding on to his basis. But leverage is one of the real benefits of real estate investing. There is virtually no other investment the average person can make where a lender would be willing to underwrite 80% or more of the cost and forego any participation in appreciation in the asset.

Income Generation

Real estate also offers the potential of rental income, from the addition of a rent-paying roommate to renting investment properties to generate income. The concept of house hacking refers to buying a home with the intent of renting out part of it to cover some or all of the expenses. Types of house hacking includes options such as renting out individual bedrooms in a property; buying a multi-unit property such as a duplex, living in one unit and renting the other out; creating a finished basement rental unit; converting a detached structure, such as a garage, into an accessory dwelling unit, as well as renting out storage room in a property.

Note:

When you rent a room in your home, you must claim the money paid to you as rental income on your tax return.

A recent drive with a schoolteacher and part-time Lyft driver in Los Angeles revealed that he was using his Lyft income to buy and lease small multi-family residential properties. Once he reaches "seven doors," he anticipates generating enough rental income to cover his loan expenses and allow his wife to retire.

The rise of short-term rental opportunities through online listings also provides opportunities for income generation from a primary residence. Local zoning codes and homeowner association rules may limit these opportunities, however.

Tax Advantages

One of the most important tax benefits that comes with owning a home is the fact that you may be able to deduct all or a significant portion of the mortgage interest and property taxes that you pay.

MORTGAGE INTEREST

If you itemize deductions on Schedule A of your federal income tax return, you can generally deduct the interest that you pay on debt resulting from a loan used to buy, build, or improve your home, provided that the loan is secured by your home. In tax terms, this is referred to as "home acquisition debt." You're able to deduct home acquisition debt on a second home as well as your main home (note, however, that when it comes to second homes, special rules apply if you rent the home out for part of the year).

For mortgage debt incurred after December 15, 2017, up to $750,000 of home acquisition debt ($375,000 if you're single or married and file separately) qualifies for the interest deduction. If your mortgage loan exceeds $750,000, some of the interest that you pay on the loan may not be deductible. Home financing obtained prior to December 15, 2017 is grandfathered into the prior law in which all interest is deductible. If you are paying interest on debt between $750,000 and $1 million related to a home loan acquired prior to that date, your deduction remains the same.

A deduction is no longer allowed for interest on home equity indebtedness (i.e., a second loan or equity-based line of credit) unless the home equity loans is used to substantially improve your home. For more information see IRS Publication 936.

MORTGAGE INSURANCE

At the end of 2017, Congress ended the ability of eligible homeowners to deduct private mortgage insurance and other qualified mortgage insurance premiums. In late 2019, Congress relented and extended the expired tax provision allowing eligible homeowners to claim the deduction for their 2018, 2019 and 2020 federal income taxes. At the time this book was written, it remained to be seen if the deduction will be extended further.

Based on the 2017 tax changes, however, the deduction is phased out if your adjusted gross income is more than $100,000 ($50,000 if married filing separately) and no deduction is allowed if your AGI exceeds $109,000 ($54,500 if married filing separately).

Qualified mortgage insurance is insurance provided by the Department of Veterans Affairs, the Federal Housing Administration, the Rural Housing Service, and qualified private mortgage insurance (PMI) providers to protect the lender from a loss if the homeowner is unable to pay the mortgage and the home goes into foreclosure. It is commonly required on loans for more than 80% of the purchase price of the property and is paid by the homeowner. Once equity in the home exceeds 20%, homeowners can be released from the need to pay the insurance.

REAL ESTATE PROPERTY TAXES

If you itemize deductions on Schedule A, you can also generally deduct real estate taxes that you've paid on your property in the year that the taxes are paid to the taxing authority. However, for 2018 through 2025, individuals are able to claim an itemized deduction of up to only $10,000 ($5,000 for married filing separately) for state and local property taxes and state and local income taxes (or sales taxes in lieu of income taxes). Previously, there were no dollar limits.

If you pay your real estate taxes through an escrow account, you can only deduct the real estate taxes actually paid by your lender from the escrow account during the year. Only the legal property owner can deduct real estate taxes. You cannot deduct homeowner association assessments, since they are not imposed by a state or local government.

CAPITAL GAIN TAX EXCLUSION

When it comes time to sell your home there is a very important advantage to home ownership — the capital gains tax exclusion. Under Section 121 of the current tax code, single people or married couples filing separately are entitled to $250,000 per person in capital gains tax exclusion from the sale of their residence on their federal tax returns. Married couples filing jointly have a combined exclusion limit of $500,000. No capital gains taxes are owed on profit from the sale of a home until it exceeds the exclusion. (While many states mirror the federal tax codes, not all recognize this exclusion. Consult your tax adviser for further information.)

To qualify for a capital gains exclusion, you must have owned and used the property as a principal residence for at least two of the five years before the sale. It does not need be your principal residence at the time of the sale or exchange. You can only take a capital gains exclusion once every two years, however, there is no limit as to how many times the exclusion may be taken.

Any time you can avoid paying taxes, you have more money to reinvest. In our prior example, if the homeowner sold his townhouse at a $50,000 gain over the original purchase price, together with his original down payment he has $100,000 to reinvest (although closing costs and Realtor fees will take a sizeable bite). At 20% down, with $100,000 he may be able to qualify to purchase a $500,000 property. If one does this every two years (you must own the home and live in it as your principal residence for a total of 24 months) it's possible to strategically move up the housing ladder steadily building equity. Another option is to use some or all of the gains to purchase investment rental properties.

Investment Property Tax Advantages

On the commercial real estate side, expenses such as mortgage interest, real estate taxes and insurance are written off against income as a cost of doing business. But there is another benefit exclusive to commercial property — depreciation. When you purchase an investment property, you can write off the purchase price against income over a certain number of years — a tax deduction known as depreciation.

In addition, taxes on capital gains from selling an investment property can be indefinitely deferred by rolling over proceeds from the sale into another investment property, or properties, with a §1031 exchange (more about this later).

Real estate investment trusts, or REITs, get an extra tax benefit in that they avoid corporate taxes by paying out most of their income as dividends.

It's possible to never pay taxes on capital gains from an investment property under the current tax law. Tactics to eliminate federal capital gains taxes on real estate include:

1.   Die and leave the property to your heirs, at which point it is "stepped up" in basis to market value, eliminating capital gains.

     •   Estate taxes could apply based on amounts in excess of the federal estate tax exemption at the time of death.

     •   State estate taxes could be due. States have individual estate tax exemptions and need to be evaluated on a state by state basis.

2. Convert a rental property to a primary residence and live there until Section 121 exclusion is effective before selling. This includes a mandatory five-year hold period. The key is your intention at the time you acquired the replacement property. Did you honestly acquire it for investment purposes? Did you have a significant change in circumstances after the acquisition which caused you to move into the property? Can you prove your intention and that change in circumstances?

If so, you may be able to re-characterize that §1031 exchange-deferred gain on investment property into gain on your principal residence and enjoy some or all of the $250,000 or $500,000 exclusion on its sale.

- Property must be your primary residence for two years of the past five years.

- Taxes will still be owed on depreciation recapture and gains may be adjusted to reflect the amount of time the property was used as an investment rental.

- Can only take advantage of this exemption once in any given two-year timeframe.

3. Combine both a 121 capital gains exemption and a Section §1031 exchange when capital gains on a primary residence exceed the $250,000 (single or married filing separately) and $500,000 (married filing jointly) limits.

- Capital gains up to the exemption limit would be taken out as "boot" in the transaction. The remaining proceeds from the sale would be rolled over into a §1031 exchange like-kind property.

- The owner would need to move out of the primary residence and establish the property as an investment. After a reasonable seasoning period, it is then possible to sell the investment home utilizing Section §1031.

- This defers taxes on reinvested gains, it does not eliminate them. However, subsequent §1031 exchanges can continue the deferral of gains as long as the property is held under the same ownership.

Caution: Always consult your tax advisor in advance to making major real estate decisions to evaluate the tax impact of selling and acquiring real estate. Very little is straight forward when it comes to determining federal and state taxes and laws are subject to change.

Portfolio Advantages

Real estate investments can also help optimize an investment portfolio's diversification.

REDUCED VOLATILITY

Solid portfolio management means diversifying your investments so that when one instrument performs poorly, another may pick up the slack.

Modern portfolio theory suggests that real estate is an important part of an investment portfolio's asset allocation. From asset allocation we get diversification, which can potentially result an overall reduction in risk.

Real estate tends to have a low correlation with stock market fluctuations and is often regarded as protection against inflation. For this reason, real estate investments may help increase your portfolio's return, or stabilize your portfolio when other assets are declining or behaving inconsistent with past trends.

INEFFICIENT MARKETS

Some investors follow the theory that the securities markets are efficient, and others do not. However, I do not know anyone who believes that the real estate markets are efficient. Inefficient markets create opportunities for smart investors to make excessive gains. What this means is that skillfully conducted real estate analysis can really pay off.

The reason why real estate markets differ from securities markets is that there is no good system for complete and accurate information exchange among buyers and sellers. There is no central marketplace such as in the securities markets, where the New York Stock Exchange or other exchanges provide continuous pricing information on every listing. Instead, real estate is traded in generally illiquid markets. regional or local in nature, where transactions are made to achieve investors' often unique investment objectives.

DIVERSE INVESTMENT VEHICLES

Adding to the attractiveness of real estate investing is the wide range of investment vehicles that can be used to invest in properties — from direct real estate ownership to investing indirectly through:

- Real estate investment trusts (REITs)
- Real estate exchange traded funds (ETFs)
- Commingled real estate funds (CREFs)
- Infrastructure funds
- Delaware Statutory Trusts (DST)
- Limited Partnerships (LP)
- Limited Liability Corporations (LLC)
- Etc.

Real Estate Investing Has Risks

Like all investments — There can be no guarantee that buying real estate will prove profitable

- Location, location, location can be the difference between a property gaining or falling in value.

- Real estate markets cycle. Purchasing property at the top of a price cycle can result in falling values and years before the property's value recovers.

- Unlike securities, there is no good system for knowing the exact value of real estate.

- Real estate markets are generally illiquid and regional or local in nature.

- Costs to sell real estate, from the Realtor's commission to improvements and closing costs, can significantly impact profitability.

- Real estate requires ongoing management.

Understanding and managing these risks is why you need to keep reading.

It's tough to make an apples-to-apples comparison of investing in real estate versus equities. But it's fair to say that real estate investments have just as much, if not more, return potential as stock investments. When you combine price appreciation, income potential, and the inherent tax benefits of real estate investing, there's potential for wealth-building, long-term returns.

Case Study: Meet Sam Zell

The son of Jewish immigrant parents from Poland, Sam Zell's start in the real estate business was managing a 15-unit apartment building in return for free room-and-board when he was in college. He was soon managing the owner's other properties and together with his fraternity brother won a contract with a large apartment development owner in Ann Arbor to manage student housing. By the time Sam graduated with a law degree from the University of Michigan Law School, he and his fraternity brother were managing more than 4,000 apartments and owned 100-200 units outright. When work as a lawyer did not turn out as interesting as the real estate field, he returned to real estate investing, initially focusing on a field he knew well — apartment buildings.

In 1968, Zell founded the predecessor of Equity Group Investments and was joined a year later by his former partner. Their small firm grew into one of the largest public real estate companies in history. Zell has a mixed history of investing (particularly outside of the real estate industry) with both successes and failure, but at the time of this writing his net worth was estimated well in excess of $5 billion. For more information, you might enjoy Zell's book, Am I Being Too Subtle?: Straight Talk From a Business Rebel, published in May 2017.

Chapter 2:

From Home to Investment

"Owning a home is a keystone of wealth — both financial affluence and emotional security."

Suzi Orman, Investment Advisor / Journalist

Individuals have typically started investing in real estate through residential properties, often opting to keep a prior house as a rental when they move or upgrade their home. There are many reasons to purchase a home beyond the satisfaction of having a place you can call your own. Studies show that homeowners tend to be happier than renters. In addition to being more satisfied with their own personal situation, homeowners also report better physical and psychological health than renters.[†] There are also very real financial advantages.

With home ownership you can:

1. Convert rent payments into mortgage payments, allowing you to build equity in the home over time as the mortgage is paid off.

2. Reduce your taxes by deducting interest on qualified home loans (up to $750,000 for couples or $375,000 if single or filing separately).

3. Increase your net worth through appreciation in the value of the home.

[†] Social Benefits of Homeownership and Stable Housing, NATIONAL ASSOCIATION OF REALTORS® Research Division - April 2012 - https://www.nar.realtor/sites/default/files/migration_files/social-benefits-of-stable-housing-2012-04.pdf

4. Recover the cost of improvements in your home by an increased tax basis when it comes time to sell.

5. Use the leverage provided by mortgage financing to increase the benefit of appreciation.

6. Shelter from taxes gains from a profitable sale of your home.

A home can become a means of forced savings as payments and appreciation add to your equity in the property. For many people today, their homes are their largest single asset and a significant source of future retirement funding. Through equity lending programs, home ownership can also provide a source of emergency funds.

Like all investments, there can be no guarantee that buying a home will prove profitable. Location, location, location have long been the difference between a property gaining or falling in value. Real estate markets also cycle. Prices go up and down, sometimes slowly and other times quickly. Purchasing a home at the top of a price cycle can result in falling values and years before your home's value recovers. Purchasing at the bottom of a cycle can be difficult if you are concerned that prices will continue falling but offers more opportunity for appreciation in a recovery.

Unlike securities such as stocks, bonds and mutual funds, there is no good system for knowing the exact value of a house. Markets for buying and selling are generally illiquid and regional or local in nature. There are costs to sell a home, from the Realtor's commission (typically 6%; 3% to the seller's real estate broker and 3% to the buying real estate broker) to improvements and closing costs, which can significantly impact profitability.

There is also the impact of the costs of home ownership on your ability to fund savings for retirement, college costs, vacations, and other financial goals.

To make certain homeownership is a benefit and not a money trap, it helps to start out with a clear idea of how buying a home will impact your lifestyle and your financial future.

Understanding the Cost
of Real Estate Ownership

	Monthly Cost	Annual Cost
Mortgage – principal and interest		
Mortgage insurance *If down payment is less than 20% of purchase price*		
HOA Fees		
Real estate taxes		
Property insurance		
Utilities		
Gas		
Electric		
Water		
Trash		
Sewer		
Telephone		
Cable/internet		
Periodic Inspections		
Maintenance		
Improvements		
TOTAL COSTS		

Real estate purchased purely for business purposes that generates income can deduct the majority of these fees from income generated by the property to determine taxable income.

If your real estate purchase will be your primary home, there are limits on the deductibility of interest, mortgage insurance and real estate taxes from your taxes. Other costs are not deductible.

With the passage of the 2017 Tax Cuts & Jobs Act (TCJA), if you itemize deductions on Schedule A, you can generally deduct mortgage interest, mortgage insurance and real estate taxes that you've paid on your property in the year that they're paid to the taxing authority. For 2018 to 2025, deduction of interest on qualified home loans is limited to a maximum of $750,000 for couples or $375,000 if filing separately. Individuals can claim an itemized deduction of up to only $10,000 ($5,000 for married filing separately) for state and local property taxes and state and local income taxes (or sales taxes in lieu of income taxes).

Comparing Buying Versus Renting

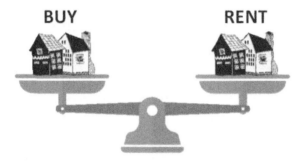

You may have run across the argument that buying a home isn't a good investment, because buying a home will typically cost more than renting a comparable property and most buyers end up paying far more in interest costs than they will experience in appreciation in value. The catch is that you need to live somewhere, so the real comparison needs to be between the costs of buying a home and renting, and how the decision will ultimately affect your net worth.

When Renting May Make Better Sense

In most cases, it is better to buy than rent. But there are conditions when continuing to rent may make better sense:

- Your rent is lower than average — and you expect it to stay that way. If you happen to have a rent-controlled apartment in a desirable part of Manhattan, you may be better off investing your savings.

- You plan on moving in a few years. Remember the costs to buy and sell a home can make short-term ownership unprofitable.

- You're in a super-expensive housing market (like Seattle, San Francisco or Honolulu).

Financial Benefits of Owning

Suppose you decide to purchase a $250,000 condominium with 15% down ($37,500) and you roll closing costs into the mortgage increasing it by an estimated $6,000. Monthly payments for a $218,500 30-year, fixed-rate mortgage at 4% will be $1,043. Adding taxes, private mortgage insurance (because your down payment is under 20%) and homeowner association dues — which will cover the majority of your insurance costs, exterior maintenance and common areas — will increase monthly payments, with the final number depending upon where the property is located. *Property taxes and insurance vary widely for different regions of the country. HOA dues will depend on the type of structure as well as amenities available for residents.*

Let's make the assumption that inflation averages 2.5%, annually increasing the value of the property, rent payments and costs for property taxes, insurance and homeowners dues by the same amount. Both the condo owner and renter pay the same utility expenses. For this example, we will assume the associated costs (taxes, HOA dues, private mortgage insurance) for the buyer start at $657 for a total expense of $1700 per month while a comparable unit rents for $1500 per month. Each year the renter's costs will increase by the 2.5%

inflation rate, while only the associated costs will increase for the home buyer.

Cumulative Costs Through Year 5*

Renter		$94,600
Home Buyer		$103,900
Interest	$41,500	
Principal	$21,000	
Associated costs	$41,400	

*Numbers have been rounded for ease of comparison

At first glance, the homeowner has paid $9,300 more for a comparable unit over five years. But the home has potentially increased in value by nearly $33,000 (2.5% annual inflation) and the homeowner has paid off $21,000 of the loan balance. Combined with the original $37,500 down payment, the individual now has $91,000 in equity. To achieve a comparable increase in value by investing the down payment of $37,500 + $9,300 in higher costs, the renter would need to earn more than 14% annually on his accumulated funds. Unlike the equity accumulated in the owner's primary residence, those gains would taxable upon sale.

The longer the individual owns the property the more cost-effective ownership will become over renting because the $1,043 mortgage payment is fixed for the term of the loan while rent costs increase each year. Once the loan is paid off, the monthly payments for the homeowner include only the associated costs.

Cumulative Costs Through Year 10*

Renter		**$201,660**
Home Buyer		**$213,300**
Interest	*$78,800*	
Principal	*$46,500*	
Associated costs	*$88,000*	

Numbers have been rounded for ease of comparison

By year 10, out-of-pocket costs for the renter are still below those of the home buyer by a total of $11,640, $2,340 of which occur in the second five years. The owner's annual costs have decreased dramatically over the last five years. In addition, provided the home has continued to increase in value 2.5% annually, the owner has gained $70,000 in appreciation, paid $46,500 in principal and combined with the original down payment now has $154,000 in equity. Which can be tapped tax free.

Building a real estate portfolio now becomes a question of how one opts to use that equity. Among the options are:

- Sell the house and use the equity to purchase a new home in a better location or with more features that might aid appreciation.

- Sell the house and split the equity between purchasing a new residence and an investment property.

- Keep the house as a rental and use other savings to buy a new residence or opt to rent a personal home for a while.

- Refinance the current house, cashing out equity to purchase a new home and keep the current property as a rental.

Naturally, we have to add the caveat that this is a hypothetical illustration only. There can be no guarantee that home prices will appreciate in line with inflation, nor that inflation will remain at 2.5% for 10 years. An uninsured event, such as a flood or earthquake could severely damage the property. Maintenance costs may increase the costs of homeownership. Every investment has the potential to lose value as well as increase in value.

Pros and Cons of Buying a Home to Convert to a Rental

There are some definite advantages to buying a home that you transition into an investment property.

1. Financing for investment properties tends to have higher interest rates and often requires larger down payments.

Most lenders consider home loans to be less risky than investment property loans. When the buyer lives in the property, they may be less inclined to walk away in the event of financial problems. Occupied properties are also less likely to be neglected and tend to be better maintained. As a result, home mortgage rates are typically lower and have longer terms, i.e. 30-year fixed-rate loans.

With any mortgage, you'll be asked to sign a legal document stating you intend to occupy the property as your primary residence for a specific amount of time (typically one or two years). You won't be allowed to turn that property into a rental before that time period is up. When the property is transitioned into a rental after the agreed upon time period, unless the mortgage contract states otherwise, the mortgage remains in place, unaffected by the change.

2. By owning a home as a principal residence for at least two of the five years before the sale, the property owner can exempt up to $250,000 in gains from capital gains taxes ($500,000 if married and filing jointly) upon the sale of the property.

Any time you can avoid taxes on gains, you have more to reinvest. This can be an enormous advantage over time. As long as you have met the two-year requirement, you can still sell the property after using it as a rental without a tax hit on gains accumulated during your occupancy. There are some catches, including recapture of depreciation taken while the property was used for a rental, so make certain and consult a tax specialist to assure that you are working with the correct data.

3. Converting your property to a rental may allow you to avoid selling during a market downturn and give the property more time to appreciate in value.

If you envision returning to the home someday, it may make better economic sense to hold onto the property and rent it for an interval rather than try to buy a comparable home in the same area years later, particularly if you have an existing low-cost mortgage.

4. If you are in a position where renting another home makes more sense than buying a new home, your former home will be generating rental income to help cover the costs of renting another home.

You might have a short-term job assignment, trial period with a new job, move to be with family members in need of assistance, take a year off to travel, etc. during which your home can be used to generate supplemental income while you are gone.

5. You will be able to write off many expenses of ownership against rental income on your taxes, lowering your taxable income. Utilities, homeowner association fees, repairs to the house, insurance, property taxes, mortgage interest and more can be deducted each year. Other potential deductions, such as depreciation, should be considered.

While your real estate purchase is your primary home, there are limits on the deductibility of interest, mortgage insurance and real estate taxes from your taxes.

Taxpayers who itemize deductions on Schedule A can generally deduct mortgage interest, mortgage insurance and real estate taxes for the property in the year that they're paid to the taxing authority. The 2017 Tax Cuts & Jobs Act (TCJA) set deductibility limitations on interest based on loan amounts. For 2018 to 2025, deduction of interest on qualified home loans is limited to a maximum of $750,000 for couples or $375,000 if filing separately. Individuals can claim an itemized deduction of up to only $5,000 ($10,000 for married filing jointly) for state and local property taxes and state and local income taxes (or sales taxes in lieu of income taxes).

There are drawbacks as well.

1.   Becoming a landlord requires compliance with local, state and federal laws, including the Fair Housing Act, which originally was intended to prohibit discrimination based on sex and race, but has become a great deal more complicated. You also need to comply with local zoning (which may require a permit to transition to rental housing), HOA requirements for rentals, etc.

2.   Owning rental housing may subject you to municipal and state limits on rent increases, the standards you set for accepting tenants and your ability to evict tenants.

3.   Insurance requirements and taxes are typically higher for a non-owner-occupied residence. One reason for higher insurance costs is the need to obtain personal liability insurance, which will protect you against being sued by a tenant. Rental property insurance may be lower since it covers the building but doesn't cover your renters' personal items. (Your rental contract should require tenants to have renter's insurance.)

4.   Successfully renting a property requires finding good tenants (including running credit and reference checks), overseeing the maintenance of the property, and assuring that it remains in good repair.

If a pipe freezes, a toilet overflows, a heater malfunctions or squirrels get into the attic, you are responsible. If you will not be available or able to handle problems, you may need to hire a management company to screen and oversee your tenants, collect rental payments, maintain the property and handle any legal issues that could come up with tenants, i.e. evicting problem tenants. This will lower your net income from the property.

Case Study: Converting a Family Home to Multiple Rental Units

Joe and Margaret purchased a large home when they first began their family. Located in a small college town, it was an ideal house for the family over the next 20 years. But with their children grown, Joe and Margaret, found themselves with more home than they needed and limited retirement savings. When an opportunity came for Joe to transfer to a new job out of state, rather than update and sell the house, they decided to convert it into a multi-bedroom rental for college students.

Over the next five years they realized $6,000 a month in rental income, enabling them to build their retirement savings. When it came time to retire, they were able to take advantage of substantial appreciation in their property due to the increasing popularity of the college and limited student housing in the area.

Chapter 3:
Make a Plan Before You Buy

"You ought to be able to explain why you're taking the job you're taking, why you're making the investment you're making, or whatever it may be. And if it can't stand applying pencil to paper, you'd better think it through some more. And if you can't write an intelligent answer to those questions, don't do it."

Warren Buffett

When you sit down with an investment professional to put together a strategy for your investment portfolio, the first step is typically an *Investment Policy Statement*. This statement includes the general rules for the portfolio, including suitable investments. It outlines the investment goals and objectives of a client and describes the strategies and limitations that the manager should employ to meet these objectives. Specific information on matters such as asset allocation, risk tolerance and liquidity requirements are included.

A *Real Estate Investment Policy Statement (RIPS)* sets the parameters for a real estate purchase whether residential or an investment property. It begins much the same as an Investment Policy Statement with an evaluation of the prospective buyer's financial situation — current savings, available funds for a down payment, income, existing debt, monthly expenses — and moves beyond the present day to the buyer's goals.

RIPS Can Save You From Making a Buying Mistake

A Real Estate Investment Policy Statement (RIPS) starts with

1. Identifying why investor is interested in acquiring a real estate investment property.

   Investor motives:

   a. Cash Flows
   b. Tax planning
   c. Appreciation
   d. Hedge Inflation
   e. Diversification
   f. Emotional
   g. Effects of leverage
   h. Geographic location

2. Establishing reasonable expectations, objectives, constraints, and guidelines in the investment of the portfolio's assets.

   a. Why are they interested in owning investment property?
   b. How long do they anticipate holding the property?
   c. What are their present and long-term employment prospects?
   d. Is their job likely to require relocation in the near future? If so, what might the timing look like?
   e. When do they anticipate retiring and how will that impact their income requirements?
   f. What are their financial goals? Are major investments coming up in the near future or the need for funding?
   g. What are their standard of living and spending habits?

Also considered are the buyer's technical skills, temperament, and repair skills. Is the individual suited to managing a property or is a hands-off approach more appropriate? Does a trouble-free property matter most or does the buyer prefer a "fixer-upper" where sweat equity will add to the value of the property?

The policy also sets forth for the investors' understanding:

- Risk aspects of real estate investing
- Defines and describes the basic determinants of value in real estate
- Encourages effective communication between the investor and his commercial real estate asset management team

Analysis of Alternative Properties

Depending upon the real estate sophistication of the investment advisor, the RIPS will also include a comparison of potential properties to determine which best suits the goals of the investor. Because Synergy has the capacity to model investment decisions, we help investors look at which property best fits their goals and at what price a purchase makes sense. Elements of the model are shown in Chapter 5.

SAMPLE RIPS

INVESTOR PROFILE:

Name	DOB	Occupation	Income	Net Worth
Jonathan Ward	12-7-66	Business Owner	$500,000	$3,000,000
Susan Ward	5-15-75	Spouse	$0	$3,000,000

Accredited Investor	YES	**Qualified Investor**	YES

INVESTOR SUMMARY:

Jonathan and Susan are interested in acquiring a real estate investment property to provide diversification to their liquid stock and bond portfolio. Their objective is to find a property that has the potential for capital appreciation and can produce both positive cash flow in the future.

INVESTOR MOTIVES:

Appreciation	Desire an increase in value over holding period.
Hedge Inflation	Desire a hedge against inflation.
Diversification	Seek diversification from low or uncorrelated returns to stock portfolio.
Emotional	Like the appeal of brick, mortar, curb appeal. Psychological security.
Effects of leverage	Desire to balance maximizing yield through leverage, with business risk.
Cash Flows	Positive net after tax cash flows if used as a rental.
Tax planning	Desire to minimize taxes on capital appreciation.
Geographic location	The West coast – Washington – greater Seattle area Safe area where Susan would feel comfortable visiting by herself late at night.

PORTFOLIO OBJECTIVES:

When setting your objectives, you also need to set both financial and non-financial constraints and goals. Often this financial goal is stated in terms of discounted cash flows (net present value) or an internal rate of return (IRR). You also need to consider how your technical skills, temperament, repair skills, and managerial talents fit a potential investment.

Return Objective	**TOTAL RETURN: Current yield plus appreciation.** Further, returns can be considered in nominal terms and in real terms. Nominal returns include inflation and real returns adjust the return without inflation. Returns can also be examined on both a pre-tax and post-tax basis, and before and after debt. Via financial modeling, scenario and sensitivity analysis, and Monte Carlo simulation, we can fully explore a range of possible portfolio outcomes. **IRR YIELD REQUIREMENT: 12% – 15%** **NPV PROFILE: POSITIVE**
Risk	Investment theory and historical capital market return data suggest that, over long periods of time, there is a relationship between the level of risk assumed and the level of return that can be expected in an investment portfolio. In general, higher risk (e.g., volatility of return) is associated with higher return. Returns can also be evaluated by comparing relative returns to absolute returns. Given this relationship between risk and return, a fundamental step in determining the investment policy for the Portfolio is the determination of an appropriate risk tolerance. There are two primary factors that affect the Investor's risk tolerance: Financial ability to accept risk within the investment portfolio and willingness to accept return volatility.

Risk (cont.)	Taking these two factors into account and based on previous inputs concerning investment time horizon and cash flow needs, the Investor rates his or her own risk tolerance as:
	Possessing the ability to seek both modest capital appreciation and income from their portfolio. This investor will have either a moderate time horizon or a slightly higher risk tolerance. While this range is still designed to preserve the investor's capital, fluctuations in the values of portfolio may occur from year to year.
	Please recognize that higher returns involve some volatility and you must have a willingness to tolerate declines in the value of your real estate portfolio.
	Risk is discussed further in the section Evaluating Risk.
Time Horizon	Your time horizon is your projected or desired time to hold your investment property. Based on financial analysis, we can determine the optimal projected time to hold the investment. As specific property characteristics and market conditions change, the time horizon (holding period) should be reanalyzed. In general, directly owned real estate investments should have a longer holding period compared to other investments.
	Capital values fluctuate over shorter periods, and you should recognize that the possibility of capital loss does exist. However, historical asset class return data suggests that the risk of principal loss over a holding period of at least 10 to 20 years can be minimized.
	TARGET TIME HORIZON: 7 YEARS
Taxes	Taxes can affect the investment policy in several ways and should be analyzed by comparing pre-tax vs. post-tax opportunities, such as:
	• The determination as to the appropriate investment vehicles for a portfolio, either taxable or tax-free, and/or income producing or growth through capital appreciation.
	• The selection of either an active or passive strategy to be employed for a particular asset class and the manner in which the property is titled.

Taxes (cont.)	Ordinary income and both short- and long-term capital gains taxes may apply.
	As a result of deferred taxation, the after-tax return on commercial real estate typically is greater than an alternative investment with a comparable before tax yield. The cost-recovery deduction normally defers (and saves) taxes, an effect that is magnified by debt financing.
	Other issues to consider with your tax counsel are the effects of suspended losses and §1031 exchange opportunities.
	CURRENT TAX RATES: **SHORT TERM CAPITAL GAINS: 39%** **LONG TERM CAPITAL GAINS: 0 – 25%** **RECAPTURE: 25%**
Liquidity	Directly owned real estate is an illiquid investment and may take several years to sell. Moreover, reinvestment into the property may require further liquidity than projected. Considerations for working capital, capital improvements, and operating shortfalls should be carefully analyzed.
	Additionally, note a difference between marketability and liquidity. Marketability indicates the fact of "Salability", while liquidity indicates how fast that sale could occur at the current price. Marketability deals with getting the property ready for sale and making the sale, while liquidity focuses on realizing cash proceeds. Being illiquid does not necessarily mean non-marketable. It may still be sellable but not quickly or without loss, or a reduction in price.
Legal & Regulatory	We recommend that you seek the advice of an attorney for any concerns you may have regarding your real estate investment property's legal and regulatory constraints.

Unique Circumstances	Marketability of Assets: Due to the Investor's relatively long-term investment horizon, the Investor has determined that this Real Estate Investment Policy Statement can be invested in illiquid, long-term investments.
	Diversification: Investment of your funds shall be limited to the following categories:
	Permitted Asset Classes
	1. Apartments- Class A&B
	2. Industrial Properties
	3. Mixed Use
	4. Office
	Prohibited Asset Classes and/or Security Types
	1. Hotels
	2. Raw Land
	3. Development projects
	4. Retail
	When and if applicable, this RIPS should reference the NCREIF property index to gain insight to property performance indicators.

The RIPS is intended to be a summary of an investment philosophy and the procedures that provide guidance for the investors and their financial professionals. These policies should reflect the investors' current status and philosophy regarding the investment of the real estate portion of their portfolio.

A RIPS is not a static document. It should be reviewed and revised periodically to ensure it adequately reflects any changes related to the portfolio, to the investors' situation, or to the capital markets.

The RIPS also states that there can be no guarantee about the attainment of the goals or investment objectives outlined herein. And that real estate brokers and consultants are unauthorized to give investment advice unless they are also a registered investment advisor. A real estate license allows the broker to bring a willing buyer and will seller together, and to assist them in completing a transaction.

In many ways a RIPS is even more important than an Investment Policy Statement because of the unique characteristics of real estate:

1. REAL ESTATE IS RELATIVELY ILLIQUID

    - Real estate can take months to get a purchase contract and more time to reach the closing table.

    - It may be difficult to sell real estate in a declining market without reducing the sales price.

    - A poor buying decision can result in a significant loss of investment and inability to sell.

    - Fractional ownership in real estate may have a planned disposition schedule, making it difficult to cash out before the investment objectives are met.

2. TO BE PROFITABLE A REAL ESTATE INVESTMENT MUST BE ABLE TO RECOUP HOLDING COSTS AND SELLING EXPENSES AND LEAVE THE SELLER AHEAD OF THE INITIAL INVESTMENT.

There are really just two ways to profit from a real estate investment — there must be sufficient appreciation to recoup the initial investment and costs of ownership when the property is sold, or the property must generate sufficient income to provide a desired return on capital.

Given this information, the RIPS establishes reasonable expectations, objectives, constraints, and guidelines in the purchase of real estate.

Simply having a Real Estate Investment Policy Statement isn't a guarantee of success. You need an investment plan. There are many ways to invest in real estate from flipping (purchasing a home that is undervalued, or whose value can be enhanced with cost-effective improvements), speculating in hot markets, purchasing a home for future conversion to a rental, or simply holding to take advantage of long-term appreciation. Regardless of your plan, if the market turns against you, you may need a time horizon of five years or more to avoid a loss. You must:

1. **Have a plan and work your plan.** Put a Real Estate Investment Policy Statement in place and use it to guide your investment decision-making.

2. **Network with like-minded individuals and organizations.** Never stop learning. By associating with individuals and organizations with the same real estate goals, you gain a flow of new ideas that might augment and hasten your financial goals. Reading industry materials and attend local workshops.

3. **Place the highest priority on protecting your assets.** Keep your real estate adequately insured. Make certain mortgage payments, taxes and bills are kept current. Use quality contractors. Think about ways your investment could be destroyed and act to prevent such disasters.

4. **Include your family in your decisions and share your knowledge.** When your family is informed about your plan and your investment decisions, they'll will be more likely to offer support and help you meet your goals.

5. **Stay educated.** Successful investors are smart investors. They're clear on their goals and how their goals serve their future. To maintain this awareness, they read and attend workshops, and are always interested in improving their knowledge and skills.

6. **Pass along what you've learned to your peers.** By talking about the lessons and information you and they have learned, not only do you help each other as friends and peers, but you open the door to improvement. This builds a trusted network of individuals who are happy to share what they know.

7. **Remain emotionally unattached to specific investments.** The only reason to stay attached to an investment is if it fits into your investment plan and is bringing you the returns you expected. Don't hold any investment longer than you should, even if, for some reason, it has sentimental value. You are invested to make money; if that's not happening at the pace you expected, sell and reinvest in something else that will bring your required rate of return (RRR).

Chapter 4:

Buying the Right Property

"I will forever believe that buying a home is a great investment. Why? Because you can't live in a stock certificate. You can't live in a mutual fund."

Oprah Winfrey, media mogul

This chapter is designed for individuals who are considering purchasing a home that they will live in and later convert to a rental property. But much of the information also applies to purchasing a home purely for your residence as well as purchasing a property for use as a rental.

You are going to need to assemble a team of real estate professionals to help you with the purchase of your property, whether a home that will be transitioned to a rental or sold to finance the purchase of an investment property, or an investment property from the start. These individuals will include your

- Realtor
- Lender/Mortgage banker
- Inspector
- Title company

In some states you may also be required to use a lawyer to complete a real estate purchase.

But before you talk to any of these professionals, do your homework. If you are buying a home with the intent of later owning it as a rental property, you need to know whether or not your home is actually rentable. Is the home appealing as a rental property? Is your intended use of the property legal?

Know the Law

One of the most important things to know buying a house as an investment property is whether there are government or homeowner association restrictions on that particular property and neighborhood that limit the ability of homeowners to rent their homes.

Second, you want to ensure that you conduct the rental of your property in a legal manner. Among the things to know before renting are the tenancy agreement to inspections, rent collection, terminations, and a basic understanding federal, state, and local housing laws in your real estate market, and what your rights and obligations as a real estate owner are.

Find the Right Property

Start by looking at the local real estate rental market and rental rates for different properties in your area. Find out what features make an income property attractive and appealing to tenants. Zillow.com can be a very useful resource when it comes to understanding the rental market.

Use the RENT tab at the top to zero in on areas of your community where you would like to own property and check the rental costs of different property types and sizes.

When you are looking for a property with rental appeal, look for access to mass transportation, job centers, recreational facilities, and community features that might appeal to a market that doesn't have the down payment or interest in purchasing a home. Remember there are always far more renters for a moderately priced rental than a "executive" home. A two-bedroom townhouse or condo can be more affordable if it allows more than one individual to pay the rental cost.

Know what you want and put together a written plan before you start talking to real estate professionals to put your plan in action. Being in control of the buying process is extremely important because there is a major conflict of interest in the real estate industry that makes it more profitable for Realtors and mortgage bankers to upsell.

When you are first starting out and looking for a home, you may be disappointed in the selection and tempted to overspend for the home you really like. Stick with your budget. There will be time and opportunity to move up in a few years if you make the right buying decision now.

Compensation Can Create Conflicts

The compensation structure of the real estate industry is rife with conflicts when it comes to the buyer's interests. Professionals throughout the real estate industry are going to make the most money the more home you buy. Once the transaction closes, so does their responsibility to the buyer. They have no vested interest in making sure your purchase is in your best interest or that it makes sense for your financial wellbeing.

A selling agent's responsibility is to maximize the selling price of the home for the seller and in the process, maximize their commission. Mortgage industry compensation is often tied to origination volumes.

The more dollars the mortgage banker loans, the greater the profit to the firm and individual salespeople. As a result, the typical advice to a buyer is simply to purchase as much home as they can afford. There is no consideration as to whether this makes sense for the buyer's overall financial situation.

Synergy Asset Management, LLC and our real estate brokerage firm, Synergy, have taken a distinctly different approach to the real estate decision, governed by our Code of Ethics.

"The Company's Code of Ethics ("Code") has been adopted to promote and maintain the highest standard of personal and professional conduct in the real estate profession. All independent agents/employees (agents) of the firm are expected to subscribe and adhere to the Code, which serves to assure public confidence in the Company and the services it offers. All agents of the firm will acknowledge, in writing, receipt of the Code and any amendments.

Each agent shall:

1. *Always place the financial interests of the client first. Agents shall recommend only those transactions that are suitable for a client, based on that client's particular circumstances and situation. If acting as a fiduciary, an agent has an affirmative duty of utmost good faith to act solely in the best interests of the client and to make full and fair disclosure of all material facts, particularly where the adviser's interests may conflict with the clients.*

2. *Disclose fully to clients the services provided and compensation received. All financial relationships, direct or indirect, or any potential conflicts of interest shall be fully disclosed on a timely basis. All client inquiries shall be answered promptly, completely, and truthfully.*

3. *Be subject to a review and monitoring procedure for personal real estate activities. Client transactions will always be given preference for execution and allocation on either sales or purchases.*

4. *Maintain the confidentiality of all information entrusted by the client to the fullest extent permitted by law.*

5. *Comply fully with all statutory and regulatory requirements affecting the delivery of real estate services to clients.*

6. *Strive to establish and maintain excellence personally and among colleagues in all aspects of real estate services.*

7. *Maintain the highest standard of personal and professional conduct.*

8. *Promptly report any violation of the Code to the firm's broker."*

Build Your Real Estate Team

Select a professional Realtor with whom you are comfortable working and whom you feel has the knowledge, integrity and experience to meet your needs. Most real estate agents sell only four to six homes a year. Few have experience with commercial or investment real estate purchases. While you may get more personalized service from those individuals, their practical experience can be limited.

A qualified real estate professional will help you view the transaction from an investment standpoint, including the following analyses.

Investment Transaction Management		
• Buyer Representation • Seller Representation • Syndication Representation		
Investment Analysis	**User Decision Analysis**	**Market Analysis**
• Identifying investment objectives • Ownership entity selection • Financing review • Investment valuation advocacy • Risk analysis • Asset management • Taxation • Acquisition strategies • Disposition alternatives	• Lease terminology advice • Space and lease comparison • Valuing leases • Comparing leasing and owning • Alternative use decisions	• Market analysis • Market research • Forecasting demand • Supply factors • Supply and demand dynamics • Gap analysis • Location and site feasibility • Modeling • Financial feasibility

A good real estate agent or buyer's broker guides you through the process of buying a home and makes the process much easier. This assistance can be especially helpful to a first-time home buyer. In particular, an agent or broker can:

- Help you determine your housing needs
- Show you properties and neighborhoods in your price range
- Suggest sources and techniques for financing
- Prepare and present an offer to purchase
- Act as an intermediary in negotiations
- Recommend professionals whose services you may need (e.g., lawyers, mortgage brokers, title professionals, inspectors)

- Provide insight into neighborhoods and market activity
- Disclose positive and negative aspects of properties you're considering

Keep in mind that if you enlist the services of an agent or broker, you'll want to find out how he or she is being compensated (i.e., flat fee or commission based on a percentage of the sale price). Many states require the agent or broker to disclose this information to you up front and in writing.

Several designations in the real estate profession indicate advanced training and knowledge:

- **CCIM — Certified Commercial Investment Member** — the wearer has completed advanced coursework in financial and market analysis, and demonstrated extensive experience in the commercial real estate industry.

- **CIPS — Certified International Property Specialist** — the designee has successfully completed an intensive program of study focusing on critical aspects of transnational transactions, including currency and exchange rate issues, cross-cultural relationships, regional market conditions, investment performance, tax issues, and more.

- **CRB — Certified Real Estate Brokerage Manager** — this certification is geared toward real estate managing broker professionals to increase their level of industry knowledge and their firm's profitability.

- **CRE — Counselor of Real Estate** — individuals recognized by their peers and clients for their high-level knowledge, experience, and integrity.

- **CRS — Certified Residential Specialist** — awarded to experienced Realtors® who complete advanced training in listing and selling.

- **MRP — Military Relocation Professional** — engaged full time in real estate and relocation services with knowledge and skills specific for the needs of active duty and retired military personnel and their families.

All Lenders are Not Created Equal

Your real estate agent will suggest sources and techniques of financing for you, but don't hesitate to shop other lenders. A mortgage is a product, just like a car, price and terms may be negotiable.

Home loans are available from thrift institutions, commercial banks, mortgage companies, credit unions and a rapidly growing market segment — online mortgage companies. Online lender Quicken Loans has become the largest retail mortgage lender in the country. Mortgage brokers arrange loans rather than lend money directly by shopping rates with multiple lenders.

Industry Rules of Thumb for Mortgage Payments

Medium Credit — the buyer can qualify for the lesser of 28% of gross income or 36% of gross income less fixed monthly expenses.

Good Credit — the buyer can qualify for the lesser of 36% of gross income or 42% of gross income less fixed monthly expenses.

Investment real estate has a separate set of parameters depending upon the property's ability to generate income, typically through rents.

Not all lenders offer the same product, nor the same pricing. Closing costs can vary by thousands of dollars. Get multiple quotes including different types of mortgages. Ask for estimated closing costs.

When you find a lender you like, find out how you can prequalify or get pre-approval on a loan. This will give you an estimate of how much you can borrow and can give you priority over other buyers because the seller will know you have the capacity to purchase the property.

Popular Types of Mortgages

Conventional Fixed Rate Mortgages

- Low risk
- 10- to 40-year terms
- Interest rate doesn't change
- Larger down payment (compared to government mortgages) may be required
- Principal and interest payment remains the same over the term of the loan

Adjustable Rate Mortgages (ARMs)

- Higher risk for the borrower because interest rate changes
- Initial interest rate often lower than conventional fixed-rate mortgage
- Interest rate may go up or down
- Interest rate usually adjusted annually
- Rate adjustments may be limited by cap(s)
- Payment caps can result in negative amortization in periods of rising interest rates — your debt increases

Government Mortgages

- FHA, VA, or bond backed
- Interest rate sometimes lower than conventional fixed-rate mortgage
- Variety of programs available
- Low down payment requirements
- Less stringent qualifying ratios
- Attractive to first-time homebuyers
- Higher insurance costs may apply for FHA loans
- Payment remains the same

Hybrid Adjustable Rate Mortgages (ARMs)
- Higher risk due to changing interest rate
- Initial interest rate often lower than conventional fixed-rate mortgage
- Fixed term for 1-10 years, then becomes a 1-year ARM
- May have option to convert to a fixed-rate mortgage before becoming a 1-year ARM
- Interest rate may go up or down
- Rate adjustments may be limited by cap(s)
- Payment caps can result in negative amortization in periods of rising interest rates

Jumbo Loans
- For 2020, any loan for a single-family home or condo above $510,400. In high-cost areas, mortgages above $765,60 are considered jumbo loans for 2020
- Size of loan increases lender's risk, so interest rates are generally higher than for conventional fixed rate mortgages

To apply for financing, you will need:
- The name and address of your bank, your account numbers, and statements for the past three months
- Investment statements for the past three months
- Pay stubs, W2 withholding forms, or other proof of employment and income
- Balance sheets and tax returns, if you're self-employed
- Information on consumer debt (account numbers and amounts due)
- Divorce settlement papers, if applicable

You'll sign authorizations that allow the lender to verify your income and bank accounts, and to obtain a copy of your credit report. If you've already made an offer on a house or condo, you'll need to give the lender a purchase contract and a receipt for any good faith deposit that you might have given the seller.

The Home Inspector

A home inspection is an essential part of buying real estate. In fact, it is so important we have dedicated an entire chapter to the inspection process.

An inspection is designed to find evident problems with a home before you buy. While the inspection can cost anywhere from $300 to $1000 or more, it is funds well spent. Your real estate agent can recommend reputable home inspectors to you, but it never hurts to check their references and get referrals from friends and relatives. You can also check online resources such as the American Society of Home Inspectors' (ASHI) Find a Home Inspector tool, which lets you search by address, metro area, or neighborhood.

Interview at least three inspectors before deciding whom to hire. Find out if they are licensed or certified (not all states require licensing); their credentials; how long they have been in the business; what exactly they check and what they do not check; and when you will see a report. Ask for a sample report to see how thorough the inspector is and how problems are explained.

Plan to be there when the inspection is held. This gives you an opportunity to learn more about the home's construction and maintenance needs and ask the inspector questions.

A typical Inspection covers:
- Heating and cooling systems
- Electrical
- Plumbing
- Interior and exterior
- Garages
- Baths
- Kitchen, which includes cabinets, counters, sinks, faucets, garbage disposals and other built-in appliances
- Insects
- Exterior walls

- Parapets, trim
- Chimney
- Foundation
- Slabs
- Basement and crawl space
- Examination of the attic and roof to assess the insulation, ventilation, framing, roof surface, flashing, penetrations, drainage, overhangs, gutters and downspouts

Legally, sellers are required to make certain repairs. These can vary depending on location. Most sales contracts require the seller to fix **structural defects, building code violations** and **safety issues**. These can be expensive repairs if you opt to forego the inspection and encounter problems later.

The Title Company

This is an area where once again, your real estate agent will have recommendations as to the firm to use. Since you are going to be paying the bill for the title company's services — and they are very important services — you want to make certain the company has a good reputation and is well managed.

The title company's primary role is to ensure the seller is legitimate and has maximum rights to sell the property through a title search, which establishes that seller is the legitimate owner and there are no outstanding issues with the property such as:

- Unpaid taxes
- Open second mortgages and HELOC loans
- Special assessments
- Judgments or demands
- Unpaid HOA fees
- Liens for unpaid taxes
- Other legal issues specific to the area

Provided no issues are found, the title company will issue owner's and lender's title insurances protecting the property owner and the mortgage company respectively from any future claims. This is paid by the buyer through a one-time charge based on the value of the property.

If a subsequent issue arises with the title, the title insurance assures the buyer that the title company is responsible for resolving the issue. For example, an estate sells the deceased's home to liquidate the asset for the heirs. Subsequently, a former girlfriend shows up with a document stating the home is hers upon his death. It is up to the title company to resolve the issue. If the claim turns out to be legitimate, the buyer must be compensated for the loss of property.

In addition, the title company will typically:

- Act as escrow agent, holding deposits and other payments until the transaction is completed
- Order the property survey
- Act as closing agent; The final closing for a home is typically held at the office of the title company
- File all required change of title documents with the state

Preparations for Purchasing Real Estate

Obtain a copy of your credit report from the three major credit unions — Transunion, Equifax and Experian. You are entitled to receive one free report each year or if you are refused credit at any time. Make certain three reports are accurate and dispute any erroneous information. This information, combined with your credit score, influences the approval of your loan application and interest rate.

You can also order your free annual credit reports online at www.annualcreditreport.com, by calling 877-322-8228, or by completing the Annual Credit Report Request Form (available on line at www.annualcreditreport.com) and mailing it to: Annual Credit Report Request Service, P.O. Box 105281, Atlanta, GA 30348-5281.

How Much Can You Afford?

According to a general rule of thumb, you can afford a house that costs two and a half times your annual salary. But determining how much you can afford to spend on a house is not quite so simple. Since most people finance their home purchases, buying a house usually means getting a mortgage. So, the amount you can afford to spend on a house is often tied to figuring out how large a mortgage you can afford.

While your mortgage broker can help you develop an idea of how much you can borrow, it is a good idea to also **work with your financial advisor or financial planner** to determine how much you should make as a down payment and how much it is prudent to borrow. Remember, compensation can create conflicts when it comes to receiving the best advice for your situation.

Determining how much you can borrow takes into account your gross monthly income, housing expenses, and any long-term debt.

Generally, if you're applying for a conventional mortgage, your monthly housing expenses (mortgage principal and interest, real estate taxes, and homeowner's insurance) should not exceed 28% of your gross monthly income. In addition, most mortgages require borrowers to have a debt-to-income ratio that is less than or equal to 43% percent. In other words, you should be spending no more than 43% of your gross monthly income on longer-term debt payments. It may be helpful to use one of the many real estate and personal finance websites to help you with the calculations.

The "rule of thumb" provides a guideline only. You need to look at your overall costs and lifestyle to make certain you are not over-extending your finances with the home purchase. The following financial worksheet is designed to you evaluate individual properties you are considering based on overall ownership costs beyond mortgage principal, interest, taxes and insurance.

Calculating the Cost of Ownership

	Monthly Cost	Annual Cost
Mortgage – principal and interest		
Mortgage insurance If down payment is less than 20% of purchase price		
HOA Fees		
Real estate taxes		
Property insurance		
Utilities		
Gas		
Electric		
Water		
Trash		
Sewer		
Telephone		
Cable/internet		
Periodic Inspections		
Maintenance		
Improvements		
TOTAL COSTS		

Know What You Want

Before you begin looking at houses, review with your Realtor the features that you want your property to have and make the buying process as targeted as possible. If you are looking for a somewhere you will live, having a safe place to live and a property that meets your needs should take priority. If you are buying for investment purposes, potential for appreciation and rental income becomes more important. Features to consider might include:

- Home price range for the given community
- Location or neighborhood
- Quality of construction, age, and condition of the property
- Style of home and lot size
- Number of bedrooms and bathrooms
- Quality of local schools
- Crime level of the area
- Property taxes
- Proximity to shopping, schools, and work

Remember that facts such as age, construction materials, location, security devices and fire protection systems, and proximity to the fire department will influence future insurance costs. Newer homes are built according to stricter building codes, and the electrical, heating, and plumbing systems are likely to be in good shape, reducing the risk of fire and water damage. Brick homes are more fire-resistant than wood frame homes. Discounts may also be available for weather-resistant features such as hurricane shutters or impact-resistant roofs.

Insurance premiums are likely to be higher for homes located near the coast or in areas at high risk for a natural or weather-related disaster. Floods and earthquake damage are not covered by a standard homeowner's insurance policy. Separate insurance will need to be purchased to cover these risks.

If you are buying in a covenant controlled, i.e. Home Owners Association (HOA) community, make certain you receive a copy of the HOA's documents in advance. Are elements of the community covered by the association — such as common areas and common exterior walls — in good repair? Does the HOA have reserves? Is it in good financial conditions or are special assessments and increases in dues likely? Are the restrictions on the use of your property and expected maintenance reasonable?

APPRECIATION POTENTIAL CONSIDERATION

An important concern when purchasing a personal home or an investment property should be its present value and potential for appreciation — i.e. increased resale value. You don't want to overpay for a property or invest in a market where home values are falling. If a situation comes up where you need to sell before you anticipated, you want to minimize the potential for a loss.

In the analysis of real estate properties, as with all investments, valuation is a key concern. Real estate offers a new complication, however, in that property values are not fixed, but rather unique to each property based on three main determinants: Demand, Supply, and the Property.

Demand stems from a market area's economic base. Property values follow an upward path when employment is increasing and typically fall when employers begin to lay off workers. For some properties, the area of greatest concern consists of a few blocks. For others, an area of hundreds of square miles serves as the relevant market area. Population demographics and psychographics (emotional dispositions) are also key elements of demand.

Supply is the competition for buyers from similar properties. The more properties on the market for a given number of buyers or sellers, the lower the value becomes. The fewer desirable properties on the market, the higher value becomes.

The Property itself is a key valuation factor. Location, location, location is critical. A great property in a poor location will lag market prices. This can be a positive for a buyer who is looking for depressed properties in areas that appear slated for rebirth, but a poor location typically means lost opportunities for profit for sellers and more difficulty eventually selling the property. The quality and attractiveness of the property, improvements made and efficiency of use, along with few restrictions on the use of the property typically impact market value.

In addition to the features of the property, you need to consider the community. If the property is in a subdivision subject to a Declaration of Restrictive Covenants that include a homeowners' association then the property is subject to mandatory membership. Before purchasing, you need to review the association's bylaws and covenants, architectural control guidelines, and financial condition of the association. It can also be useful to look at the legal history of the association. Are lawsuits common? If you have issues with any of the homeowners association's requirements or structure, do not complete the sale. There is always another property.

Your real estate professional can help by providing a comprehensive analysis of the areas in which you are interested. This includes average sale prices over the past eight years and the trend of price change. This can give you a sense of the appreciation you might be able to achieve based on how long you plan to own the house, how well you maintain the property and any upgrades you decide to make to the property. Several factors outside your control may also influence the value of your property, however, including the real estate cycle as well as a multitude of economic, political, and environmental changes.

The investment caution that past performance is not an indication of future return very much applies to real estate investments. As with all investments, to limit risk you need to understand the investment and factors that could adversely affect it.

Your Real Estate Investment Policy Statement helps provide price, payment and purchase parameters that guide the selection of your new home in the context of your overall financial situation.

Applying for a Mortgage

Mortgage Preapproval vs Prequalification

Once you have an idea of how much of a mortgage you can afford, you'll want to shop around and compare the mortgage rates and terms that various lenders offer. When you find the right lender, get preapproval for a loan.

Preapproval is when the lender, after verifying your income and performing a credit check, lets you know exactly how much you can borrow. This involves completing an application, revealing your financial information, and paying a fee.

Prequalifying gives you the lender's estimate of how much you can borrow. In many cases. The estimate can be made over the phone, usually at no cost. Prequalification does not guarantee that the lender will grant you a loan, but it can give you a rough idea of where you stand. If you're really serious about buying, however, you'll want to get preapproved for a loan.

Generally, if you're applying for a conventional mortgage, your monthly housing expenses (mortgage principal and interest, real estate taxes, and homeowners insurance) should not exceed 28% of your gross monthly income. In addition, most mortgages require borrowers to have a debt-to-income ratio that is less than or equal to 43%. That means that you should be spending no more than 43% of your gross monthly income on longer-term debt payments.

It's important to note that the mortgage you qualify for or are approved for is not always what you can actually afford. Before signing any loan paperwork, take an honest look at your lifestyle, standard of living, and spending habits to make sure that your mortgage payment won't be beyond your means.

Before You Apply

Do some homework before you apply for a mortgage. Think about the type of home you want, what your budget will allow, and the type of mortgage you might want to apply for. Obtain a copy of your credit report, and make sure it's accurate. If there is any erroneous information, you'll want to dispute the information with the credit bureaus and the company reporting inaccurate information and quickly correct it.

Be prepared to answer any questions that a lender might have of you and be open and straightforward about your circumstances.

What You'll Need When You Apply

When you apply for a mortgage, the lender will want a lot of information about you (and, at some point, about the house you'll buy) to determine your loan eligibility. Here's what you'll need to provide:

- The name and address of your bank, your account numbers, and statements for the past three months
- Investment statements for the past three months
- Pay stubs, W2 withholding forms, or other proof of employment and income
- Balance sheets and tax returns, if you're self employed
- Information on consumer debt (account numbers and amounts due)
- Divorce settlement papers, if applicable

You'll sign authorizations that allow the lender to verify your income and bank accounts, and to obtain a copy of your credit report. If you've already made an offer on a house or condo, you'll need to give the lender a purchase contract and a receipt for any good faith deposit that you might have given the seller.

Finalizing the Application

As your mortgage application is processed and finalized, your lender is required by law to give you a Loan Estimate within three business days of receiving your application. The Loan Estimate is a form that spells out important information about the loan you applied for, such as the estimated interest rate, monthly payments, and total closing costs for the loan.

Closing the Purchase – What to Expect

The purchase process has four basic steps

- The Purchase and Sale Agreement (the offer)
- The Acceptance
- The Inspection
- The Closing

Once a property is selected, negotiation begins through the purchase and sale agreement or the formal offer contract. This document outlines the terms of the offer including price, earnest money amount, and closing date. Most home sale offers and counteroffers are made through an intermediary, such as a real estate agent. All terms and conditions of the offer, no matter how minute, should be put in writing to avoid future problems.

Once agreement is reached between the buyer and seller, a mutually accepted contract will be completed and sent to escrow, and the buyer will be required to deposit their earnest money. This is typically a nominal payment that will go towards your purchase when the sale is finalize. The amount of the payment is dependent upon the property and circumstances.

Typically, your attorney or real estate agent will prepare an offer to purchase for you to sign. You'll also include a nominal escrow payment that will go towards your down payment when the sale is finalize. The amount of the payment is dependent upon the property and circumstances.

If the seller accepts the offer to purchase, he or she will sign the contract, which will then become a binding agreement between you and the seller. For this reason, it's a good idea to review any offer to purchase in detail with your real estate agent before you sign. Because most contracts are standardized by state, you typically do not need to have an attorney review it, but if you have any questions or are uncertain about any conditions, review the contract with your legal counsel. Buying a home is one of the biggest purchases you will ever make. Take your time, ask for a second opinion if needed before you sign anything with which you are uncomfortable.

A number of additional stages now begin:

- Final financing is arranged including a professional appraisal of the property.
- A formal property Inspection is conducted by a professional, licensed home inspector hired by the buyer to protect the buyer's interest in the property and to assure there are no

costly surprises after the purchase closes. An acceptable inspection should always be a condition of the purchase offer and a point at which the purchase can be canceled without penalty if significant issues are found.

- The title company researches the property to assure that a clean deed is available and there are no encumbrances, liens or undisclosed easements against the property. Title insurance is typically required to provide the buyer with recourse should there be a problem with ownership of the property.

Chapter 5:
The Home Inspection

by Todd Livingood

The last thing you want to do as a buyer is fall in love with a property and be willing to overlook its problems. A home inspection is your reality check. After the closing, it's too late to discover costly problems with your new home.

Because this is so important in making the right purchase decision, we asked Todd Livingood to provide the professional inspector's view of the process. Todd has been a professionally certified inspector since 1999 by Inspection Training Associates, Oceanside, CA. He has more than 20 years of experience performing residential home inspections and has performed commercial property inspections for over 17 years. His firm, Livin Good Inspections, is based in Kirkland, Washington and performs inspections throughout a wide service area in Washington state.

One of the main reasons why you want to have an inspection on property you are purchasing is to determine the condition of the building in its current state. The older the building, the more likely potential problems exist. A common mistake people make is assuming that new construction is built to perfection and is flawless. This assumption can be very far from the truth.

Why Have an Inspection?

Determining the condition of the building is quite important in knowing whether there is anything major that needs to be repaired, or something that could lead to major issues with the house. Clearly, one of the most important things is identifying potential safety hazards and conditions that can affect your liability. If you are a landlord renting the property, you can be liable to your tenant. If you are a homeowner, you could be liable for accidents that happen to guests or visitors. An example is a lack of handrails on stairs or a deck that doesn't have railings. If a deck with railings already exists, are the slats close enough to prevent small children from getting stuck, or worse, falling?

As you've heard a thousand times before, we live in a litigious society, so you when you buy a property you want to identify safety hazards. You can correct them to limit your liability, and if you are occupying the property yourself, you want a safe environment for your family.

It's not uncommon to find safety issues that need to be resolved in both new and old structures before you move in. Such things as exposed electrical wires or loose stairs need to be fixed right away. Even if you're moving into a refurbished home, it's wise to also determine the age of major appliances and systems so you can know the estimated replacement time frames and costs.

Anticipate Maintenance Costs

Knowing how old your furnace and water heater are, and how many years are left for your roof's viability are important so you don't get surprised with an unexpected and unplanned cost. Most inspectors can give you a good idea of the ballpark expenses but are not required to quote actual prices. As a landlord or a homeowner, you should know what your costs are going to be over the next three to five years.

Identifying deferred maintenance items is also important. You always want to keep an eye on your costs and plan for them. Here in the Northwest, where we get a lot of rain, exterior house paint is important and can be a large cost. If your home has southern exposure, that part of the house will get a lot of sun deterioration. This can cause your siding and trim to crack or warp, and your caulking to shrink and separate, which can lead to water entry and damage.

The larger the house, the bigger the paint job is going to be. It's not uncommon to spend between $5,000 - $9,000 on an exterior paint project. Depending on your location, within three to four years of the house being built, rotted trim on the exterior has probably already taken hold. It's also likely that there is water intrusion that needs to be addressed. Most homeowners are not checking their exterior walls and repairing around windows, doors, drains, wall trim, wall penetrations, and so on.

Use Inspection Information to Negotiate Price Reductions

If you're buying a home, you can use inspection information to negotiate a price reduction. Experienced buyers know what to look for and they know the price for repair, so they might be able to talk the price down quite a bit. Many buyers get a home inspection solely with the intent of finding problems they can use to negotiate the price down because they're going to do a full remodel anyway.

A home inspection could uncover foundation issues, settlement issues, drainage problems and even wood-boring insect activity in the wood structure underneath the house. Inspectors hate to be the bearer of bad news when someone has found their dream home, but better that than get stuck with a lemon. This is why a home inspection is so important.

There is also a lot to be said for simply having peace of mind and knowing what you're buying, rather than wondering if you got a good deal or are going to regret your purchase. For the typical person, the largest single expense they'll ever make is buying their home, so having professionally evaluated information is truly sensible. The alternative is living in a home that could ruin you financially over the next 15 or 20 years. It's nice to know what you're buying. You wouldn't buy a brand-new car without giving it a test drive, and it's even more imperative to have a mechanic look at a used car before you buy it.

No Inspection is Often a Costly Error

As surprising as it might seem, there are people who actually try to avoid having a home inspection. This is especially true with people who are purchasing a new construction because they're operating under the assumption that there is nothing wrong with their new home. It was just built, right? It just passed inspections, right? First-time home buyers don't see value in having a home inspection and are about to spend so much money on the purchase of the house that they don't want any additional costs. Since the lender is not going to require a home inspection, first-time buyers don't get one. The new buyers have had to pay money for an appraisal and closing costs, so if an expense is not required, they prefer to pass. They can save some money and maybe buy some extra furniture instead. Of course, they are missing a chance to, in effect, purchase meaningful insurance in the form of a home inspection; but they are preferring to pinch pennies, which could cost them more in the long run.

Home buyers can also be vulnerable in hot markets. If the market is hot, the seller may not be willing to allow pre-inspections. The seller knows their house is worth a lot of money and the property may even be in a bidding war. People will purchase a house without an inspection because they feel they have to, if they want the house. So they waive an inspection and buy the property without knowing what they're really buying. This is a form of Russian roulette in the real estate market. Not everyone is lucky enough to fire a blank chamber.

Inspections Can Be a Good Tool for Sellers

On the other hand, sometimes sellers will take preemptive action and get an inspection done before they put their house on the market so they know the condition of their home and to strengthen their negotiating hand. In this case, the seller can choose to fix something prior to putting the home on the market or have a clear idea of what the cost would be should the buyer attempt a negotiation. Knowing their home's strengths and weaknesses, the seller can price the property accordingly and operate from a strong hand. They can be completely transparent, and everyone is fully informed about the property's value. This strategy also takes liability off the seller because they are disclosing what they know. No one needs a lawsuit, and this gives everyone, both the seller and the buyer, peace of mind.

Inspections Vary Based on Real Estate Type

All real estate is classified as either residential, commercial, industrial, or raw land. Residential real estate can be either single-family homes, condominiums, townhouses with or without homeowners' associations, and co-ops.

Also classified residential property is multifamily dwellings such as a duplex, triplex or a quadplex.

Commercial properties are shopping centers, strip malls medical and educational buildings, hotels and offices, and apartment buildings with five units or more.

Industrial real estate consists of manufacturing buildings, warehouses, and similarly used properties.

Raw land is self-explanatory and the property could have timber, minerals, surface water, wildlife, and other types of resources. In some cases, the location of the property is valuable because it can be used for cell phone towers or advertising, so, in a sense, even the air above a property could have value.

COMMERCIAL VS. RESIDENTIAL INSPECTIONS

There are significant differences between commercial and residential real estate. Realtors are required to have two different licenses because the properties are sufficiently distinct, but in either case, you want to have a state licensed inspector analyzing the property.

Even though there are state licensed inspectors, not every inspection is equal. Some home inspectors believe they know how to do commercial inspections and they treat a commercial inspection like a residential inspection. Of course, this is not the correct approach and they are not doing what is required. When you contract for an inspection, you must make sure the inspector has experience and proceeds in a bona fide manner.

Part of the problem is that there is no commercial inspector licensing program, and as long as an inspector has a license for home inspections, he or she is legally qualified to do commercial inspections as well. It's likely this will change in the future after several significant lawsuits create enough pressure to make legislative changes. However, for now, be aware that not all commercial inspections are conducted in the best manner possible.

There are some businesses that specialize in commercial property inspections and when you look at the credentials of their inspectors, you'll see they are mostly licensed engineers that serve as part of a team of inspectors. You'll find structural engineers and electrical engineers working together on a commercial inspection.

Surprisingly, there aren't many professional associations that offer educational classes on commercial property inspections. The International Association of Certified Home Inspectors recently created a commercial division and began offering classes and a certification process, but this is rare.

Residential inspections are performed in accordance with the state's standards of practice. There are professional associations that also have standards of practice that are in accord with the state's standards of practice. One of these organizations is the American Society of Home Inspectors. They provide guidelines for home inspectors to follow. Then there are commercial inspections which are typically referred to as Property Condition Assessments, or PCAs, which perform inspections using the American Standards for Testing and Materials (ASTM). The ASTM standards have existed for a long time and are followed by engineers as well. Other organizations exist as well, like the Certified Commercial Property Inspectors Association that provide a baseline standard for inspectors to adhere to. CCPIA's vision is to strive to enhance the commercial property inspection profession by providing its members with online training and resources for the purpose of professional development and improvement.

One of the big differences between inspecting a residential or a commercial property is that the purchaser of a residential property has a lot of emotion wrapped up in the purchase. They're very sensitive to the process because this is going to be their home, and their family's home, for decades. Commercial property buyers are looking at the purchase simply as a business transaction, and typically it's a group of purchasers buying a commercial building, so they are not moved by emotion at all. For them, it is simply a sound business transaction. A home inspector has to be sensitive to the emotional context of the inspection. Both the buyer and the seller have a lot of emotions attached to the outcome.

Another key difference between a residential inspection and a commercial inspection is that as far as the standards of practice are concerned, a residential inspection does not require recommendations for repairs. The inspector is not required to give cost estimates or life expectancies of specific components of the property. There's a difference between noting the age of a component compared with knowing its life expectancy, and this subtle detail can be significant when estimating anticipated future repairs or replacement. A gas furnace can run upwards of $5,000 to replace, and a roof replacement on a typical 1,500 square foot rambler averages around $10,000. This can have a significant impact on a homeowner's funds.

If you're having a home inspection, this is likely to be information you would like to know. A home inspector will not do it as a matter of practice, but if a homeowner asks, most inspectors will gladly comply. Even so, if you're really serious about knowing the cost of repairs or replacement, your best strategy would be to contact a contractor and get a more refined estimate of the cost. When you ask a home inspector to calculate the cost, you could get a quote that varies by 20% - 40%. A home inspector can only give a quote based on their experience, and it may not be relevant to the actual costs prevalent in the market at the time.

What Inspectors Are Looking For

A married couple that is about to buy their first house always wonders what an inspector is looking for. Most inspection reports can range from 30 pages to about 70 pages long and can be very comprehensive. There is a long list of what the inspector is required to investigate, and the most important focus is on damage to house components.

Specifically, when it comes to house components, we're referring to siding, the roof, the framing of the house, plumbing systems, electrical systems, mechanical systems, windows and doors, the attic, the crawlspace, and the foundation. An inspector is required to look at all of these components.

An inspection is a visual inspection, and at no point during the inspection are holes cut to inspect hidden areas. An inspector will inspect only what he or she can visually see. Inspectors are not required to move furniture or heavy items to look behind them. The sole task is to look at the components visually, look for the proper installation of systems, operate these systems using normal operating controls (in the case of a furnace, water heater, etc.) and make professional determinations based on what is seen. In the Northwest, moisture and ventilation are significant issues because of the moisture level and humidity here when compared with inspecting a house in Texas, for example. Because houses are built so airtight these days to meet energy efficiency requirements, ventilation has become more and more important over the years.

Indoor mold is becoming more of a problem, as well. Mold wasn't as big a problem previously as it is now and that's because houses are built so airtight. Energy efficiency requirements are high and as houses are built more airtight, which means sealing against any air leaks and relying more heavily on mechanical ventilation. There was at one time more natural ventilation of houses. Now, when you take a shower, it's critically important you get that moisture and humidity out of the house. There's also a lot of moisture when cooking and doing the laundry, so it's much more important to eliminate moisture because otherwise mold and mildew will multiply.

I've been asked about homes being built during the summer when the framing is exposed to summer rainstorms and the Tyvek, which is a moisture barrier, is not yet placed. People wonder if the framing and wall structures are going to retain moisture and depreciate the quality of the exposed materials. However, no matter how much rain a building is exposed to, the wood typically will dry and there will be no compromise of the quality of the building. The framing can get sopping wet and completely saturated, but once the house is covered up, the framing dries out.

Even if the framing doesn't dry out fast enough naturally, contractors will bring in heaters or fans to dry out the wood. The building has to go through a municipality inspection and the building inspector will question circumstances that suggest improper construction.

A house inspector will also investigate whether or not the house systems were properly installed. Are the heating and plumbing units installed according to code and safety? In today's modern homes, air-conditioning systems are becoming more common in our area and they need to be properly installed as well. Often, system installation techniques can vary between service companies and even technicians within the same company. These variations may present issues or concerns that an inspector can identify and then recommend correction. As technology develops, an inspector's knowledge must also expand to be effective.

Always a major concern is safety and fire hazards. Long ago, before there were housing codes, safety and fire issues caused a lot of deaths and injuries. Safety codes and fire codes today are very protective of residence and commercial properties, and an inspector will compare the physical property against the expectations of safety and fire codes.

Another area of focus are the home's appliances. An inspector will check to see they are all functioning properly. This might include the stove and oven, the refrigerator, microwave, the dish-washing machine, the laundry machines, the furnace and water heater, and any other appliances in the house, though inspectors are not required to test some of these.

A category everybody needs to pay attention to are pests and insect infestations. There is a very distinct difference between pests such as rodents and bees, and wood destroying organisms. WDOs are termites, carpenter ants, specific varieties of wood boring beetles, etc., that require a specific state license for inspection. Not all home inspectors are state licensed for Wood Destroying Organisms. You can expect your house inspector to report on pests or nuisance insects, but unless they are state licensed for WDO, their report will only indicate a problem that needs resolution, specifically the need for a WDO Inspector or further evaluation by a licensed pest control company.

The next area of concern for a house inspector are structural issues and seismic proofing. You need to make sure your home is structurally adequate and that the foundation, framing, and roof will not collapse or is otherwise compromised. The northwest U.S. is in an area with the threat of seismic activity, and building codes protect inhabitants, as much as possible, from earthquakes and potential volcanic activity. While these codes may not be sufficient in the event of an extreme event, a house should be up to code to provide legitimate safety.

Another key area is house insulation for energy efficiency ratings. Again, there are codes that require the contractor to properly insulate a house, both to keep the owner's heating bills within reason, and also to conserve the demand for electric and gas heating resources.

An inspector will focus on house systems to determine if they are lacking proper care, maintenance, or servicing. Some homeowners get careless or lazy and don't invest the time and money to maintain their home's systems properly. This can lead to inefficient performance and, in the case of a furnace, fireplace or wood stove, can compromise a home's fire safety. Debris on the roof and in the gutters needs to be cleaned out, soot build-up in wood-burning appliances needs to be periodically removed, the caulking around windows and doors must be sufficient, and plumbing and electrical components must be operating properly. These are the main features that a house inspector will investigate.

Inspection Tools and Equipment

Home inspectors often use a variety of tools to perform a property inspection. Some of these tools are basic, like screwdrivers to remove covers from furnaces or electrical panels, and to inspect wiring and breakers. We also need flashlights to inspect large surfaces and little corners such as when we go into dark spaces like the attic, or crawl spaces. Most home inspectors will also use cameras to take photographs of deficiencies and other items that should be noted in the report. With the current level of technology, a cell phone camera is easy, convenient and even a little better than a regular camera.

A variety of electrical testers are employed when conducting a home inspection. The very basic one is the receptacle tester. It plugs into an outlet and will determine whether an outlet is wired correctly, or if it's reverse-wired, or ungrounded. If it's a specialty outlet such as a GFCI device (ground fault circuit interrupter), there's a test button that will trip the device to make sure there is proper safety protection at the kitchen outlets, at bathroom outlets, at garage outlets and exterior outlets. An inspector tests to make sure the home has safety protection at any receptacle or outlet in an area close to water where it's required by code.

Inspectors also use voltage detectors. If there is a bare wire or circuit that's sticking out, such as in an unfinished basement when we see a coiled wire that doesn't terminate properly, a voltage detector, or what is called a voltage sniffer, will be used. This device will tell the inspector if the wire is live or not, which is obviously a significant safety concern and one which will feature prominently in the report. An amp probe or amp meter is used when testing an electric furnace; these devices determine whether the furnace's heating elements are drawing a proper amperage and operating properly. With a gas furnace or oil furnace, the inspector will often conduct a test for carbon monoxide with the carbon monoxide meter. This meter is also good for checking other gas appliances in the house. When conducting an inspection, if an unsafe level of carbon monoxide output is identified, the inspector can shut the power off at the breaker because the appliance is no longer safe to operate, and they will likely contact the listing agent or the utility company. This is called "red tagging." Obviously, an inspector is unwilling to assume professional liability by allowing the appliance to continue running. A carbon monoxide meter is invaluable because when it comes to immediate personal safety, being able to identify a significant concern is paramount.

Home inspectors also use moisture meters. There are several different types on the market. There is a pin style meter which can be poked into the surface of a wall, leaving only really small pinhole marks. Some inspectors prefer using a surface moisture meter because this will not cause any damage to surface coverings. Moisture meters are great for identifying moisture inside walls or floors, especially in bathrooms and kitchens near plumbing fixtures such as sinks, toilets and showers. A moisture meter gives the inspector a snapshot of what could be hidden and unavailable to his or her eye. Normally, an inspector will look for water stains on the ceiling or in a garage that's under a bathroom or directly below a roof. Stains identify whether there is any potentially active leaks, but not all leaks make visual stains.

When it comes to gas leaks, a home inspector's nose is usually a very good tool. As you know, the utility companies add a unique additive like the smell of rotten eggs (Mercaptan) so everyone can identify a gas leak. Usually the inspector will detect a gas leak near a furnace or around the main gas meter outside the house. Then the inspector will confirm the leak with a leak detector to narrow the location of the leak. Sometimes an inspector will also use soap bubbles! This is Old School, but soap bubbles are effective with locating an actual leak on a gas line.

Another important tool is the infrared thermometer which uses infrared technology to determine temperature. This device shoots a concentrated laser beam to take a spot temperature reading on the surface of something that's not reachable by an inspector. For example, if an inspector is in a room with a vaulted ceiling, like in a living room or master bedroom, and the inspector wants to take a temperature reading of the ceiling register when the furnace is operating, it's very hard to get up there and feel the airflow coming out. This test is necessary to determine if the register has any blockage. An infrared thermometer can take a reading from a distance that heat is actually flowing from that register.

An inspector might also use a laser distance meter that serves as a fancy ruler or measuring device so the inspector can quickly measure a room or the distance from one point to another with laser technology instead of a tape measure.

Inspection mirrors are also a great tool to help the inspector with looking behind equipment or to identify combustible gases that might be spilling out of a gas water heater, for example. When there is a draft hood on an old furnace or water heater, an inspection mirror can show signs of invisible gasses spilling out of the flue instead of drafting properly. In some ways, a home inspector is like Sherlock Holmes, acting as a house doctor.

In the Northwest, we have a lot of homes that use wood stoves. With a wood stove, safety is the first issue. The location of the wood-burning device is very important because a wood stove can get up to 700°+. Wood-burning stoves are usually located close to an interior or exterior wall, so it's important they have a proper firewall behind and below them, and to make sure there is proper clearance from the flue pipe both in the room, and where the flue penetrates the ceiling and roof through an attic. The flue pipes must be checked to confirm they are properly connected and don't end up with smoke or condensation that can gather in the house.

A wood stove must be checked to make sure there are proper gaskets on the door, that they seal properly and that the stove has proper combustible air. The liners inside need to be checked also, and they are hidden most of the time. A home inspector might check the flue liners from the roof if there's access or get a visual from inside the wood stove. A recommendation might be made to have the wood stove cleaned and inspected by a professional.

Another issue is when a home is completely dependent on electricity and the power goes out. A wood stove is a great natural resource for heat, and are unlikely to ever become antiquated, but when a house doesn't have a wood stove, someone in a family might bring a propane heater or gas heater into the house, something that might be from their camping equipment This is the reason why it's become federal and state law to require carbon monoxide alarms. When you're burning a propane stove in a house for supplemental heat until the power comes back on, you can produce carbon monoxide and families have died from lack of proper ventilation.

Some homeowners install a generator outside the house to keep the house supplied with energy during a power outage. I can't recommend one heat source over the other. Both can be expensive to install. The cost could be $5,000 to $10,000, so from a cost-saving perspective, generators are probably the less expensive choice. However, there are some issues with generators. They can be noisy and many people prefer to run them in their garage, which can be just as dangerous as having a vehicle running in your room. Proper ventilation is always a big concern, a top priority. This is why it is so important to have a carbon monoxide alarm in the house. Effective ventilation is usually only achieved through mechanical fans and people are unlikely to open their windows when it's cold outside.

In the event of a power outage, your home's gas water heater should continue to function, allowing you to have hot water for the house and take hot showers, which is a big comfort. The steam will also heat up the bathroom which is very nice. Even so, new technology is moving away from tanks and toward tank-less units which will not run when there is no power since they are digitally controlled.

Most Common Inspection Flaws Discovered

The most common problem we find during an inspection is wood rot. Wood rot is due to the weather patterns we have in the Northwest because of the amount of rain we have and how moist it is in this area. Whether it's cedar, a treated wood or a non-treated wood, it's still going to rot. Decay and damage is likely to happen to wood sidings, trim, decks, and stairs. Treated wood has a preservative solution applied to it and it's treated to withstand rot and decay, but this protective feature only lasts so long. Like anything, over the years it will eventually break down and rot. The reason there is so much of this problem in the Northwest is because of the quantity of forests in this area and wood is one of the least expensive and readily available materials used to build houses.

One way to protect your home is with rainwater control. This is your gutter and downspout system, and the subsurface drains. Controlling rainwater is imperative in the Northwest. There are a variety of soil conditions with areas in the low-lying valleys, along the sandy coastlines, and up in the mountain ranges where there is a preponderance of rock and clay, or sandy loamy soil. Loamy soil is good for drainage, but in an area with a lot of rock and clay, water can gather or run in directions that cause problems. Water can pool in crawlspaces, even under new construction after one or two years if the water is not being properly routed to street drains. In some cases, the construction crews on new building projects have had to install sump pumps and redo the drain systems in crawlspaces. It has been a big problem for builders in this area.

Another common problem is overflowing gutters. If the gutters aren't kept clean, sheets of water can flow over the gutter systems and when that water hits the ground, it splashes up against the house creating water collection and water damage. When water falls steadily in one area, it can cause soil compaction and that can jeopardize the soil support for foundations and cause the foundation to crack and settle. Rainwater control is an important part of properly maintaining your home.

Roof defects are another important issue in the Northwest. When it's not raining, there aren't a lot of problems. A dry roof is a great roof when there's no rain, but when it rains nine months of the year and your roof has deficiencies, they can be compounded and lead to major issues. You can get mold, and water damage inside a wall. Keeping your roof in good condition is a real big consideration, especially when you have a heavily wooded lot. In the Northwest, a lot of houses are built on forested properties and when trees are growing close to houses, and limbs are not trimmed away from the roof lines, damage can occur to your gutters and maybe to your siding. Sometimes the wind will cause a tree limb to grab hold of the roofing material, and that can also be a big problem in a storm.

Frankly, it doesn't matter whether there is light rain or heavy rain. Sometimes a roof leak can be created in a windstorm, and even a small leak can cause tremendous damage.

You might find this interesting. A researcher discovered that if you added up all the little holes in the exterior of your home, in places such as at the edges of windows, or under or around the doors, and added them all up, you'd be able to roll a basketball through the composite hole! This is worth thinking about because older construction didn't have to be airtight, but today the newer houses have to meet energy efficiency requirements. Any time you mount a television on an exterior wall by drilling holes, you're allowing a little bit more air and heat transfer to occur in the walls.

As airtight houses are being built to meet energy efficiency requirements, the concern about mold has become more paramount. Proper ventilation has become more and more critical. Most people don't realize how dirty their exhaust fans are and how important it is to keep them clean. Most homes have exhaust fans in bathrooms, the kitchen, and the laundry room, and these fans are seldom cleaned. An inspection will often show very fuzzy ventilation shafts, and when this dust collects, it reduces the efficiency of getting air out of the house. Usually when a person first moves into a new home, a steamy bathroom only takes about 15 minutes to air out, but over the years it takes a half an hour to get all the steam out of a room. The fan blades are filthy, the exhaust fan is filthy, and the ducts are filthy, and the exhaust system is not working efficiently anymore. A homeowner can clean their exhaust fans by disassembling it and cleaning the fan blade with a can of compressed air, like you might do for your computer. All you have to do is clean it enough to make it work efficiently again, an easy task to accomplish.

Mold is a big issue, and there are literally hundreds of mold varieties. The most common type of mold here in the Northwest seems to be your standard household mold. If you don't leave your fan running for an extended period of time to get moisture out of the room, you'll probably get mold and mildew that starts to form on the ceilings or around windows. One solution is to attach timer switches to your fans so they will run for half an hour when you're done to get moisture out of the room and turn off automatically to conserve electricity.

Another place where mold can form is around sinks. When the caulk gets old, you'll see a little bit of mold and mildew on them. The industry has come out with new technology that has an anti-mold or antifungal composition for caulking. Even paints are on the market that also resists mold and fungi.

Of course, mold and fungi can also grow in the attic. Sometimes an inspector will notice that a person has had their house repainted, but the painters have painted the louvered vents shut, so even though you're turning your fan on, is not having any effect. The fan is running but the air is not moving. On other occasions, an inspector will find that louvers are missing and birds will build nests there. Bees, hornets and wasps can also harbor inside vent assemblies creating blockage. Ventilation is important, and if it is not done properly, there can be cascading problems.

Another problem homeowners face is the presence of rodents in attics and crawl spaces. In my experience, about 80% of homes in the Northwest have some sort of rodent activity. Bats are not usually an issue, but mice and rats are. Bats might be in the barns or outlying sheds, but mice and rats will be in the house. In twenty years of inspecting, I've only come across bats in attics or chimneys four times.

We have two basic types of rats in this area. We have roof rats and Norway rats. Both of these varieties are believed to be introduced to North America from abroad via ships, however, the NW does have its own native species. The ground dwelling and the larger of the two species in the Norway rat, which you'll typically find in crawlspaces. The other is the roof rat that dwell in the trees. If trees are not trimmed away from the house, rats have easy access on to the roof and can usually enter your attic. The attic is a very convenient place with insulation that makes great bedding. It's an easier life for them!

In the crawlspace, rats usually have a good water source. Sometimes there is a small plumbing leak down there, so the animals have water, and if you have a bird feeder in the backyard or dogs you don't pick up after, rats and mice can have a heyday. Yes, it's disgusting to think about, but for these rodents, poop is a food source. As for the bird feeders in the backyard, a lot of birdseed ends up on the ground, and when that happens, you are ringing the dinner bell for rats and mice. That's why it's so important to keep your attic and crawlspace rodent-proof. Pest control companies are always dealing with rodents in houses.

Of course, we have farms, both cattle and horse farms, and rat activity occurs a lot in farming areas. When you have areas of new construction, the forest where the rodents live is being destroyed. The rodents choose to live where they have always lived except now they're in your attic or crawlspace. When we build a new development, we're forcing them out of their natural homes and into concentrated human areas, so of course they're going to try to find someplace to go. This situation is exacerbated by the fact that when it comes to rodents, mice only need an opening the size of a dime to enter your home, and rats only need the size of a quarter. If a rodent can squeeze their skull through a hole, their whole body can also fit through.

Underground drains are a good access point for rodents. Usually drains don't have a screen on them, and that's where rodents can tunnel underneath the foundation. It's quite common. Another access point is the root system on wooded properties. When a tree is cut down, usually the contractor leaves the root system intact underneath the ground, and that root system usually travels underneath your home's foundation. It may take 20 years for that root system to decay but when it does, if the soil doesn't collapse, it's a nice little conduit and rodent trail. Now the rodents can travel right into the crawlspace. In Chinese astrology, the rat is known for flexibility, adaptability, and cleverness, and clearly that's for a good reason.

Another common problem are electrical outlets that are not wired properly. If someone bought a home that was built in 1960 or 1970, you'll see that old almond-colored outlet which was the style then. If they've been replaced with new white ones, that's a telltale sign that they may not be wired correctly and need attention. As an inspector of

20+ years, I know that the one outlet I don't test out of the many that I did check, will be the one that has a defect. This is the reason I don't rely on sampling.

Defects that Increase Landlord Liability

When a landlord is renting out property, tenant safety and landlord liability is a key concern. A certified inspector will carefully check everything for safety, including improper handrails and guardrails on stairs, decks, porches and balconies. These can lead to injuries, especially for young children. Landlords need to protect themselves completely so it's essential that all safety features are up to current codes. These codes don't change very often so landlords typically won't find themselves in violation of new codes, but it's more likely that the property is not meeting the existing code and needs to be properly upgraded.

The Washington State electrical code requires Ground Fault Circuit Interrupter protection for all outlets located on the exterior of the building, in the garage, in the kitchen and bathrooms, at jetted tubs and hot tubs and some other area-specific locations. In general, these are required for any electrical supply that is near a water source, and it must be protected by a GFCI device. AFCI (arc fault circuit interrupter) breakers are now required for all 15 and 20 amp branch circuits providing power to outlets in family rooms, dining rooms, living rooms, dens, bedrooms, closets, hallways, etc. Basically, any outlet that is considered accessible. These breakers protect bedroom outlets that have the potential for children to stick something into the outlet. Obviously, all outlets need to be childproofed. Now there is a three-prong outlet and child safety outlets that are required.

Another area for landlord liability is the presence of mold. With the increase in allergens, food allergies, allergies to weeds and trees, people appeared to have become more sensitive to environmental influences, and mold allergies are a big concern. This, of course, connects with improper ventilation issues. If your house has a lack of ventilation, or water intrusion, it is quite probable that there is mold growth inside the walls and closets, under kitchen fixtures, in the bathroom, and so on.

Duct work is also a source of water leaks and you could have mold growing inside your ducts. Every time your furnace kicks on, you are circulating those mold spores throughout the entire house. Water damage can also lead to molds as well as structural damage.

Oil-based paint is another issue. Some paints have potentially hazardous materials that can be ingested by toddlers. Sometimes a landlord will have a closet that contains all the materials needed to do maintenance on their property, so clearly, this closet must be securely locked to prevent child intrusion.

In older construction, popcorn ceilings contained asbestos, and asbestos could be in old duct tape or old heating vent systems, on pipes in an unfinished basement or even in ceiling or flooring tiles. When these materials begin to deteriorate, asbestos fibers can become airborne and create a potential health hazard.

Insufficient lighting in stairwells or on the outside of the house can cause accidents when people trip and fall down. Some jurisdictions have codes to ensure properly lit areas to avoid these kinds of accidents, and if the landlord is remiss with keeping up with the local code, he or she is risking exposure to liability and a lawsuit.

Another key area is the lack of maintenance on decks, patios, stairs, and walkways. All these items can become damaged and cause accidents with people falling on slippery surfaces that have algae growth and become super-slick. Another issue is tree root growth that causes surfaces to up-heave and make walkways uneven. If anybody trips and breaks a limb, a very unpleasant situation will surface along with the tree root.

Landlords need to be proactive with protecting their tenants, their property, and themselves from unnecessary lawsuits.

If an inspection turns up problems with the property, the buyer has to make the decision whether to request repairs from the seller, ask for price concessions or walk from the deal. **Don't fall in love with a flawed property. There is always another option.**

Chapter 6:
Finalizing the Purchase After Due Diligence

After due diligence is completed, the buyer and their selling broker formulate a response to fulfill contingency requirements.

1. Approve and move forward with original offer.

2. Withdraw and cancel the entire offer. This must be within the terms of the accepted contract for the potential buyer to receive a refund of the escrow deposition.

3. Counteroffer. The counter could include a price reduction, request for repairs or improvements, a seller credit to pay for some issue found in the property or any combination of the above.

After the seller has accepted your offer, you, your real estate agent, or the mortgage lender will get busy completing procedures and documents necessary to finalize the purchase. These include finalizing the mortgage loan, appraising the house, surveying the property, and getting homeowner's insurance. Typically, you would have made your offer contingent upon the satisfactory completion of a home inspection, so now's the time to get this done as well.

Given negotiations are successful, a final walk through of the property is held prior to closing to confirm that any repairs required as a result of the inspection have been made, and that there has been no damage to the property or removal of items included in the sale.

The Closing

The closing meeting, also known as a title closing or settlement, can be a tedious process — but when it's over, the house is finally yours! The closing may require some or all of the following entities to be present: the seller and/or the seller's attorney, your attorney, the closing agent (a real estate attorney or the representative of a title company or mortgage lender), and your real estate agent and the seller's agent.

Depending on what state you live in, all parties may be required to attend the closing at once or the closing may take place over the course of several weeks. Some closings can be conducted by mail or via the internet.

During the closing process, you'll receive and/or sign a variety of paperwork, including:

- Closing Disclosure: Lists all of the final terms of the loan you've selected. Your lender is required to send you the Closing Disclosure at least three business days before the actual closing meeting.

- Promissory note: Spells out the amount and repayment terms of your mortgage loan.

- Mortgage: Gives the lender a lien against the property.

- Deed: Transfers legal ownership of the property to you.

In addition, you'll need to provide proof that you have insured the property. You'll also be required to pay certain costs and fees associated with obtaining the mortgage and closing the real estate transaction.

Verify Payment Instructions Before Wiring Funds

When making your payment you need to exercise extra care to make certain your funds are transferred property. Many closing agents no longer accept certified checks due to fraud but require wire transfers of funds. Unfortunately, hackers are well aware of the increasing use of wire transfers and one of the latest email frauds involves wire transfers, in particular, wire transfers made to title companies to close on real estate transactions. In fact, wire fraud has become the fastest-growing form of real estate cybercrime in the United States.

Hackers access the title companies' computers and records of upcoming home closings or intercept outgoing emails and then email fraudulent wire transfer instructions to buyers. The email references the title company employees the buyers have been working with and even includes phone numbers (direct to the hacker) to verify instructions. Even the email address may appear to be from the title company. Once the money is wired, there is little the buyers can do to retrieve their funds. The purchase collapses and the buyers lose not only their down payments but also potentially earnest money and the upfront expenses they have incurred as part of the purchase.

Ironically, wiring money is often required in the home buying process because cashier's checks have become subject to fraud. Using a mobile banking app, unscrupulous buyers can re-deposit a certified check into their own accounts just before handing it over to the title officer. The title company may not be notified of the bad check for days or even weeks.

Given the title company requires a wire transfer, how do you protect yourself?

1. Do not assume that the email you receive with instructions is legitimate. Call the title company — using phone numbers you have obtained in person or on verified paperwork — to verify that the wire instructions you've received are correct.

2. Consult your real estate agent. They deal with the title companies and closing requirements on a regular basis and may be able to arrange acceptance of a cashier's check or assure wire transfer instructions are correct. It is in their best interest that your real estate purchase is successful.

IF YOU MAKE A FRAUDULENT WIRE TRANSFER, in some cases, particularly, if the bank still holds the transfer amount, you can attempt to reverse it. If the money has transferred, it is gone. You have no recourse, no recovery options.

Case Study

Nick and Autumn were both successful young professionals with homes that they purchased as individuals when they met. Nick owned a single-family home in a depressed neighborhood that was starting to see gentrification, with new businesses and young professionals moving into the area. Autumn's home was a two-bedroom condominium in a developed community with stable values. Although they wanted to live together in a larger home, Nick was reluctant to sell his house given his expectation that it would appreciate significantly with the neighborhood recovery. Autumn's condominium would easily rent for more than her current payments, providing cash flow.

Rather than sell either property, they decided to pool their savings and with their combined incomes purchase a third property together. Nick was able to rent his house, offsetting his mortgage costs; Autumn's condo provided income to help pay their new mortgage and they were on their way to becoming real estate investors.

Walk Through — Buyer's Journey

The following is a process Synergy built and refined to maximize value, minimize taxes, and to keep you in control when buying real estate properties.

1. **Meet with a professional**
   There's no commitment required on your part for the initial meeting. It will be educational and help you identify the next steps.

2. **Discovery Assessment**
   Our Discovery process identifies and prioritizes your buying requirements and integrates with your financial goals. *STRATEGIC PRICING — As difficult as it may be, it's important to review the market analysis and consider your home price objectively.*

3. **Financing**
    Synergy will work with you in finding the right lender helping to get you "Pre-Approved," equipping you to present your strongest offer.

4. **Finding the right home**
    When it comes to location, price, schools and style, we help you find the home that is "just right" and is aligned with your real estate investment policy (RIPS). *SHOWINGS — We will preview homes that meet your criteria, and then show you the few that meet your needs. We repeat the process until we find your ideal property.*

5. **Making an offer**
    Synergy will assist you in pricing, preparing, presenting and negotiating the "right" offer — all the way to signing the contract.

6. **Under contract**
    At this point, you and the seller have agreed to all the terms of the offer and both parties have signed the agreement. *INSPECTION — Buyers should always perform a professional inspection of the home. You may require the seller to make certain repairs. Your agent will explain all of your options regarding inspection.*

7. **The transaction**
    Synergy will be with you the entire process — Monitoring dates and deadlines while communicating with you, the lender and the other broker along the way.

8. **Closing**
    This is the transfer of funds and ownership. Congratulations!

Make sure to bring I.D. for signing. Any funds due need to be delivered by wire or cashier's check

Critical Date Checklist ✓

Seller:	Seller File: ☐
Buyer:	Buyer File: ☐
Property Address:	
Escrow Company:	Escrow Phone:
Escrow Officer:	Email:
Co-Op Agent Name:	Company:
Phone:	Email:
Co-Op Agent Assistant:	Phone:
Email:	Closing Date:

ACTIONS	DEADLINE	DATE COMPLETED	✓
Loan Application Deadline			
Contract Acceptance Deadline/Time			
Earnest Money Deposit Deadline			
Inspection Deadline			
Inspection Resolution Deadline			
Sellers Property Condition Disclosure Deadline			
Title Document Delivery Deadline			
Title Review/Objection Deadline			
HOA Document Delivery Deadline			
HOA Document Objection Deadline			
Appraisal Objection Deadline			
Appraisal Resolution Deadline			
Loan Approval Deadline			
Closing Date			
Buyers Possession Date			
Listing Start Date			
Listing Expiration Date			
Existing Home Sale Contingency			

NOTES:

Chapter 7:

Analyzing Alternative Properties

"Before you start trying to work out which direction the property market is headed, you should be aware that there are markets within markets."

Paul Clitheroe

When you are purchasing a home, your main priority is whether or not it is somewhere you want to live. Do you like the features of the house, the neighborhood, the surrounding amenities such as schools and shopping, and its proximity to work and fun? What improvements do you envision to make the property more suitable? Yes, you want to be able to afford the property, but the character of the house and area have a higher importance with respect to which property you select.

If you are purchasing a property with the long-term goal of turning it into an income-producing property, the numbers matter.

Integrating Financial Analysis in the Real Estate Decision

At Synergy, we take a very numbers-oriented approach to the real estate decision starting with the return you need to realize from your investment. We've built an extensive model that allows us to evaluate different properties based not on square feet or physical characteristics, but rather on the long-term potential of the property in terms of rental income, use of leverage, expected costs, ability to inflation-proof income through rising rents, tax implications, anticipated appreciation, and other data-driven factors.

To understand our approach, it helps to understand our firm's background. Synergy Mergers & Acquisitions is the real estate affiliate of Synergy Asset Management, LLC, a fee-based asset management firm specializing in personal wealth development and protection. Our professional focus is on analyzing investment opportunities for clients to build efficient portfolios designed to allow them to meet their financial goals. In my role as Chief Investment Officer and lead portfolio manager for SAM, I am responsible for analyzing current and potential investments for the firm through deep fundamental analysis, researching industry trends, speaking to industry experts and through a thorough understanding and application of quantitative methods and technical analysis.

Real estate is among the alternative investments we recommend for clients for many of the reasons cited at the beginning of this book. But our approach to real estate investing is very much that of the financial analyst. We want to select and hold high quality investments that meet our clients' return objectives and manage the risk of the investment underperforming.

Date	2/1/20			
General Assumptions			**Purchase Assumptions**	
Depreciation Base % of Purchase Price	60.00%		Purchase Price	$1,000,000
			Down PMT	20.00%	$200,000
Depreciation Years	27.5		+ Acq Cost	$0
Depreciation	$21,818		+Loan Points (% of Loan)	0.00%	$0
Required Return	12.00%			
Reinvestment Rate	2.00%		Total Investment	$200,000
Finance Rate	0.00%			
			Cap Rate at Purchase	5.17%
NPV	$20,583			
IRR	13.46%		NOI at Purchase	$51,700
Mod IRR	12.93%			

		Quick Value	
Suspend Losses	0	Target Cap	5.17%
(No=0, Yes=1)		Value	$1,000,000

The model analyzes several different factors of the financial decision. By modifying variables shown in blue, we can evaluate an investment under different scenarios to develop a comfort level with the potential risk of the investment and its ability to meet targeted return rates.

Loan Assumptions

Loan Amount	$800,000
Annual % Rate	5.00%
Term Years	30
Base year	2020
Prepayment Penalties — % of Loan	0.00%
Monthly Payment	$4,295
Annual Payment	$51,535
Coverage Ratio	1.00
LTV	80.00%

Operating Assumptions

Gross Rent	$80,000
Vacancy & Collection Rate	5.00%
Management Fee (% of rent)	10.00%
Tax Rate	22.00%
Rent Increase Rate	3.00%

Expense	Dollar	Increase
Utilities	$5,000	3.00%
Property Tax	$8,000	2.00%
Insurance	$2,400	0.00%
Trash	$800	0.00%
Repairs/Maintenance	$0	3.00%
Promotions/Adv	$500	0.00%
Reserves	$0	3.00%
Operating Expenses	$0	3.00%

Sales Assumptions

Property Appreciation Rate	3.00%
Selling Expense	8.00%
Tax Rate on Sale	15.00%
Recapture Tax Rate	25.00%
Sale Year (End)	8
Selling Year Cap Rate	5.00%
Selling Year NOI	$65,085
Capitalization Method	$1,344,799
Appreciation Method	$1,266,770
Cap Rate Based on Appreciation Method	5.14%

Quick Purchase Price Calculation

Purchase Price $1,000,000

IRR 10%		IRR 12%
IRR 15%		**IRR 20%**

IRR & Down Payment Data Table

Down Payment	IRR
10%	**18.56%**
15%	**15.43%**
20%	**13.46%**
25%	**12.08%**
30%	**11.06%**
40%	**9.64%**
50%	**8.70%**

The next step is to look at annual income, expenses, income taxes, after tax cash flow and selling year valuation. We want to understand what potentially is happening on a year-to-year basis. This can assist with planning when to sell or exchange a property, what return the property owner might receive in the event liquidation is required ahead of schedule, or to anticipate the impact on income of major repairs or updates. We also project where the property will be each year with respect to mortgage amortization and potential sales price.

Real estate investing has its share of risk, as has been reviewed in prior chapters and will be repeated again. When you make an investment in real property, the more information you can evaluate and analyze up front, the better the decisions you will make with respect to understanding alternative properties and which property will best meet your investment objectives.

This level of analysis also plays an important role in determining the right price for a property. When we present our analysis to property sellers who have overpriced their properties, it is much easier to justify a lower offer and more likely the offer will be accepted.

Chapter 8:

Renting Your Property

"Real Estate is a commodity bought and sold every day. Just like a stock, you would buy from your broker. The difference is, if the value of my Real Estate goes down drastically, I still have a tangible security. If my stock plummets, all I have is a piece of paper."

Rico Vecc

This chapter is designed to walk you through the process of becoming a landlord and renting your property. Even if you decide to use a professional property management firm, **read this chapter**. Assigning responsibility to a management firm does not get you off the hook if problems arise later. You need to know what the responsibilities of the management firm are, if they are acting in full compliance with the law, and whether or not your interests in the property are being protected.

If you have purchased a property with the intent of initially making it your primary home for the first few years and then converting it to a rental property make certain you have met occupancy requirements before renting.

In your original loan agreement, you will very likely find requirements that you live in the home for a certain length of time to qualify for a residential loan. If, in the future you will want to take advantage of the residential tax exclusion on capital gains, you must have owned and used it as a principal residence for at least two of the five years before the sale.

Join Your Local Landlords Association

If you are new to renting your property or have been a landlord for some time, one of the best resources you may find for keeping up with industry resources and changes is your local landlords' association. These non-profit organizations provide their members with great resources, information, and deals with providers such as Home Depot.

The **Landlord Association** is a popular real estate association that offers its members detailed information, resources, and connections one needs to succeed, "such as news, tips, tricks, great advice, and top-of-the-line services." — www.landlordassociation.org

The **National Association of Independent Landlords** provides members with information regarding how to find the best, and most reliable tenants possible, information regarding their rights and responsibilities as landlords, as well as links to additional resources.

State apartment associations provide landlords, specifically of apartments, with information regarding their rights and responsibilities, resources and networking opportunities. Some offer benefits such as discounted tenant screening, rental forms, property management education, and newsletters.

The **National Real Estate Investors Association (REIA)** is a non-profit real estate association that is a franchise composed of real estate investor groups across the country. The association represents the interests of approximately 40,000 investors, including members of Property Associations, Landlord Associations, Investor Associations, and Apartment Associations.

Know the Laws

In our last chapter on buying the right property, we stressed the importance of ensuring that you conduct your investment in a legal manner. Among the things to know before renting are the tenancy agreement to inspections, rent collection, terminations, and a basic understanding federal, state, and local housing laws in your real estate market, and what your rights and obligations as a landlord are.

As the property owner, you have obligations as to the safety of your tenants. Are you required to provide a lead paint disclosure? Do you need to provide information on registered sex offenders in the area or crime statistics? Do you have proper fire, gas and carbon monoxide monitors? Check with the Department of Housing and Urban Development for all federal landlord tenant laws, and specifically research the Federal Anti-Discrimination Law, Federal Housing Law, and Fair Credit Reporting Act. Contact your state and municipal authorities for local legal requirements.

What Can You Charge for Rent?

There are no hard and fast rules for rental rates. Rent is determined by what the market will bear for your location and property features. A number of online sites can be referenced to find out how comparable properties are listed for rent. These include sites such as Zillow.com, Trulia.com, Rent.com, Craigslist.com and more. Look at rates for your specific area. Tour properties to compare housing quality and amenities.

Just as in determining house value, location, location, location matters for rentals. In addition to the desirability of your location, you need to consider local restrictions. Some states limit what landlords can charge for rent, security deposits and late fees. Rent control laws exist, for example, in places like New York, Maryland, California and Washington D.C.

If your rent rate is higher than the market, you could end up with longer time periods between renters as you wait for someone who is willing to meet your price. Too low of a rate and you may be leaving money on the table as well as attracting less qualified tenants.

While your objective should be a positive cash flow, there may be times when losing a little money can be more desirable than losing a lot. For example, a construction project next door may make your property less desirable to rent during construction. Rather than accept a lower rent and lower quality tenant where there is potential for damage to the property, it may make sense to accept a short-term loss.

Understand Your Costs

With that said, you do need to understand the financial costs involved and whether or not you will have a positive or negative cash flow at the end of the day. In the table below we show both the Landlord and Renter costs. If the property is not rented, those costs will need to be paid by the landlord. It is also prudent to build in a reserve for legal costs in the event of a problem tenant.

In multi-family properties, such as a condominium association, some utilities may be paid through the HOA. If utilities are in the tenant's name, there should be a process in place to monitor whether or not they are being paid on a timely basis to assure that a disconnect does not result in damage to the property.

Calculating the Cost of Rental Real Estate Ownership

	Landlord Monthly Cost	Renter Monthly Cost
Mortgage – principal and interest		
Mortgage insurance If equity is less than 20% of purchase price		
Real estate taxes		
Property insurance		
Property management firm costs		
HOA Fees		

Utilities		
Gas		
Electric		
Water		
Trash		
Sewer		
Telephone		
Cable/internet		
Maintenance		
Repairs		
Legal fees		
TOTAL COSTS		

Have a Property Management Plan

Do you have the ability to manage the property on a day-to-day basis? Do you want your tenants to call you in the middle of the night with a problem? All of the negatives of home ownership are still with you when you convert your home to an income property from periodic maintenance requirements to emergency repairs but this time, they may come with late night calls and damage accentuated by neglect.

Managing the property yourself may save money, but make certain you can handle tenant demands and have resources such as plumbers, electricians and contractors you can call in for repairs.

You may want to contract with a property management company or individual to handle your rental. If you try to manage your own property without the ability and time to do so, it could end up costing you much more than what a property manager might charge. Generally, a property manager will charge approximately 50% of the first month's rent when a new tenant moves in, 8 – 12% of the monthly rental value of the property for the remainder of the lease, plus expenses. Some companies charge a per month flat rate.

A property manager will typically:

- Advertise for new tenants
- Sign leases
- Collect the rent
- Keep track of finances
- Schedule maintenance repairs
- Issue legal notices
- File evictions (you pay lawyer fees)

Even if you opt to use a property management firm, there are a number of decisions you need to make beforehand to assure that the property is managed the way you wish, starting with your rental policies and lease.

Develop Rental Policies, Write a Lease.

Most states have a standard lease contract that you can find online, but you will need to adapt it to your situation and property. Specifically, you need to set policies for your tenants.

If your property is part of an HOA, the association will have specific policies that apply to all residents, including noise levels, parking restrictions, use of common area facilities, prohibited activities, pet policies and more. Your lease should require compliance with community policies. If your tenants violate these policies, you are the one responsible for fines and penalties. Your lease needs to have a means of enforcing compliance with the HOA's requirements.

Plus, you have some decisions to make about your rental policies. While standard leases typically prohibit any illegal and business activities on the property there are issues you need to address:

- What do you require for a security deposit?
- How many people are to occupy the unit? Is there a limit on how long guests can stay?

- Is smoking allowed? This applies not just to tobacco but also legal recreational drugs.
- Will you allow pets? If yes is there a pet deposit and care requirements?
- Who will do the lawn care?
- What is the process if a tenant wants to break a lease?
- Are waterbeds allowed? What about large aquariums?
- Are there restrictions as to modifications tenants can make to the property?
- What are your inspection requirements?
- Will you allow month-to-month tenancy at the expiration of the lease? If so, what are the terms?

Review as many lease agreements as you can to find loopholes you may have overlooked. Remember each state has different rules and laws that govern the landlord-tenant policies in that state. There may be a standard lease contract required by the state or specific terms. If this is the first time you have developed a lease, consult with a lawyer to make sure your lease is legal and enforceable. Paying for a review up front can be a lot less expensive than legal fees when you are facing a problem.

Marketing Your Rental

Just like selling a house, renting a property requires attractive photographs, listings of amenities and community advantages, and key lease terms. Stage your property if need be to have attractive images to post with for rent listings. If repairs are needed to make your property more attractive, remember that this is a rental not your home. Focus on durable, easily cleaned, and low maintenance. Repairs and upgrades should be done with a cost/benefit approach and to minimize repair and service calls

Twenty years ago, you would have to rely on classified ads and For Rent publications to reach potential tenants. Today listing your rental home on online marketplaces such as Craigslist, Zillow, Trulia and Rent will reach a broad selection of potential renters looking in your specific area. There are also commercial sites where you can reach specific audiences for a fee. The online sites can provide photographs and details about your rental and even help you screen and rent your property. Plus, you can use the links to let friends and colleagues spread the word on your rental.

Do NOT put the address of your property in listings. Force people to call or email and talk with you first.

While yard signs are a useful way to market your rental, they also let everyone driving by know that the home is vacant, which may be a risk you do not want to take.

Screen Potential Renters

Most initial contacts will be by phone or email. You don't want to waste your time with applicants who will not qualify, so in your reply state key criteria, such as:

- Gross monthly income must equal approximately three times or more the monthly rent.
- Must have a favorable credit history.
- Must be employed and be able to provide proof of the required income.
- Must have good references concerning rental payment, housekeeping, and property maintenance from previous landlords.
- Number of occupants limited to two per bedroom (per state law).
- No pets (if that is the case).

CAUTION — Individual municipalities may have their own screening criteria, limiting the use of criminal checks, references, income standards, etc. Know your local regulations.

If those conditions are not a stumbling block to the applicant, offer to provide an application and suggest potential times to show the property. Do not waste time on individuals who cannot meet your qualifications.

Meet the tenant in person. Stick to your terms if they have questions. Give an application to every single person who is interested to ensure you will not be charged with discrimination. If they are interested, provide a copy of your lease for their review.

Process applications on a first-come, first-served basis. If someone doesn't qualify, move on to the next. When you deny an applicant, clearly document your reasons for why you are denying them to avoid discrimination complaints. Always inform the tenant with written notice.

In advertising and screening potential tenants, Federal law defines *seven protected classes of people that you cannot discriminate against, which includes a person's race, skin color, sex, national origin, religion, disability or familial status.* You cannot even ask questions about these terms without appearing discriminatory. You can discriminate on the basis of their financial history and ability to pay.

Be wary of trusting your personal reactions to the applicant. Always check references and employment and use an independent tenant screening service for credit and background checks. For example, TransUnion Credit Bureau offers an online SmartMove tenant screening service that verifies and provides property owners and management firms with the tenant's credit check, criminal, eviction, and Income Insights reports. SmartMove tenant credit checks use ResidentScore to predict rental eviction risk, helping landlords make a more confident rental decision.

There is a charge for the credit check that you can have the applicant pay (another sign of the seriousness of their intent to lease) or you can pay for the credit check as a cost of doing business. In very competitive markets, some landlords charge applicants up to $100 to screen their qualifications.

On the application, ask for at least three references and call each person on the list. Questions to ask include: How long have they known the individual? Would they consider them reliable? Do they meet their commitments? Do they take care of their property and living spaces? Do they have pets?

Confirm their employment. Call the employer to be sure they still work there. Ask the applicant for a few months of paystubs to make sure their income can cover the rent.

If an applicant challenges your decision not to lease to them, having an independent third-party score that indicates potential problems and employment issues provides you with a defense against a discrimination charge.

Rent only to the best tenants. A great tenant can provide years of financial security and tranquility. A bad tenant can mean years of stress and financial loss. Never accept a subpar tenant to help them out. If an applicant has a history of late payments, prior evictions filed or carried out, bankruptcy, or recent criminal or bad financial history, don't rent to them. Your financial security is at risk. Minimize the chance for loss.

If you accept an applicant, but they request that you hold the property for a limited time, require a nonrefundable deposit to do so. This deposit can be used to apply to their security deposit upon signing the lease and paying the initial month's rent and security deposit. The signed *deposit to hold agreement* details the transaction:

Received from *tenant name*, $ *amount* as a deposit to hold *property description*. The applicant has until *date* to sign a lease agreement. If not signed by that date, the deposit will be forfeited to the landlord.

Finalize the Rental Agreement

Ideally, schedule a time for your new tenant to meet with you at the property and walk them through each provision in the lease. Have the tenant initial each page of the lease agreement and important provisions — such as no pets — and sign where required. A signed copy should be provided to the tenant for his/her records while you keep the original for your files. Accept the security deposit and initial rent payment in certified funds, such as a money order or a cashier's check.

Provide a signed acknowledgment that the security deposit has been received. You legally owe your tenant the security deposit refund at the end of the lease, provided there has been no damage to the unit, so put it in a separate account where it is clearly designated as a security deposit. Some states require this by law and may also require interest paid on the account.

Document the condition of the property at the time of lease signing with photographs and a description the condition of the property. Have the new tenant walk the property and note the condition of each room and any damage. This protects both you and the tenant when it comes time to move out. When the lease if over, you will want to be able to prove whether or not any damage to the place took place during tenancy.

Establish how rent will be paid each month, whether through direct deposit, certified funds, such as a money order or a cashier's check, PayPal or other method. Will invoices be sent each month or email reminders?

Provide the tenant with your contact information in the event of any problems. Make certain you have current contact information for the tenant as well as an emergency contact.

Now you can hand over the keys and let the tenant take possession. Your job is by no means done, but you have a tenant and your property will begin producing income.

Sample Application to Rent

SAMPLE

I. APPLICATION TO RENT

THIS SECTION TO BE COMPLETED BY APPLICANT. A SEPARATE APPLICATION TO RENT IS REQUIRED FOR EACH OCCUPANT 18 YEARS OF AGE OR OVER, OR AN EMANCIPATED MINOR.

1. **APPLICANT** is completing Application as a (check one) ☐ tenant   ☐ tenant with co-tenant(s) or
   ☐ guarantor/co-signor. Total number of applicants _____

2. **PREMISES INFORMATION**
   Application to rent property at _____("Premises")
   Rent: $_____ per month + electric and gas utilities
   Proposed move-in date _____

3. **PERSONAL INFORMATION**
   a. FULL NAME OF APPLICANT _____
   b. Date of Birth _____
       (For purpose of obtaining credit reports. Age discrimination is prohibited by law.)
   c. Driver's License No. _____State _____Expires _____
   d. Social Security Number (optional) _____
   e. Phone Number: Home _____Work _____Other _____
   f. Email _____
   g. Name(s) of all other proposed occupant(s) and relationship to applicant
       _____
       _____
   h. Pet(s) (number and type) _____
   i. Auto: Make _____ Model _____ Year _____
       License No. _____ State _____ Color _____
   j. Other vehicle(s): _____
   k. In case of emergency, person to notify _____
       Relationship _____
       Address _____ Phone _____

   l. Does applicant or any proposed occupant plan to use liquid-filled furniture?
       ☐ No   ☐ Yes   Type _____

   m. Has applicant been a party to an unlawful detainer action or filed bankruptcy within the last seven years?
       ☐ No   ☐ Yes   If yes, explain _____

   n. Has applicant or any proposed occupant ever been convicted or pleaded no contest to a felony?
       ☐ No   ☐ Yes   If yes, explain _____

   o. Has applicant or any proposed occupant ever been asked to move out of a residence?
       ☐ No   ☐ Yes   If yes, explain _____

SAMPLE

APPLICATION TO RENT — PAGE 2

4. RESIDENCE HISTORY

Current address_____	Previous address _____
City/State/Zip_____	City/State/Zip _____
From _____ to _____	From _____ to _____
Landlord/Manager name _____	Landlord/Manager name _____
Landlord/Manager phone _____	Landlord/Manager phone _____
Do you own this Property ☐ No ☐ Yes	Do you own this Property ☐ No ☐ Yes
Reason for leaving current address _____	Reason for leaving previous address _____

5. EMPLOYMENT AND INCOME

Current employer_____	Previous employer _____
City/State/Zip_____	City/State/Zip _____
From _____ to _____	From _____ to _____
Supervisor name _____	Supervisor name _____
Supervisor phone _____	Supervisor phone _____
Employment gross monthly income $ _____	Employment gross monthly income $_____
Other income information _____	Other income information _____

6. PERSONAL REFERENCES

Name _____ Address _____

Phone _____ Length of Acquaintance _____ Occupation _____

Name _____ Address _____

Phone _____ Length of Acquaintance _____ Occupation _____

Applicant understands and agrees that: (i) this is an application to rent only and does not guarantee that applicant will be offered the Premises; (ii) Landlord or Manager or Agent may accept more than one application for the Premises and, using their sole discretion, will select the best qualified applicant, and (iii) Applicant will provide a copy of applicant's driver's license upon request.

Applicant represents the above information to be true and complete, and hereby authorizes Landlord or Manager or Agent to: (i) verify the information provided; and (ii) obtain a credit report on applicant and other reports, warnings and verifications on and about applicant, which may include, but not be limited to, criminal background checks, reports on unlawful detainers, bad checks, fraud warnings, employment and tenant history. Applicant further authorizes Landlord or Manager or Agent to disclose information to prior or subsequent owners and/or agents.

Applicant _____ Date _____ Time _____

Return your completed application to _____

Questions to Ask References:

Personal References

- Are they reliable?
- Do they meet deadlines?
- Retain employment?
- Take care of their living spaces?
- Have pets?

Job References

- How much do they currently make?
- How long have they worked there?
- Is this job considered temporary?

Prior Landlords

- How long did the tenant rent from you?
- What was their monthly rent?
- Did the tenant give proper notice when vacating?
- Did the tenant receive back their security deposit?
- Would you rent to this tenant again?

A Bad Rental Scenario

A real estate investor's greatest threat is sometimes the good intentions of government. A lack of affordable housing in some of America's most expensive cities in which to own real estate might seem a boon to landlords with properties to rent. In moves that seem destined to limit future housing, some states and cities are targeting landlords as the villains and limiting their ability to manage properties prudently.

Josephine owns a rental condominium in a complex that has a high percentage of renters. State rent control laws limit increases in rent to 5% plus the rate of inflation. Landlords are prohibited from evicting tenants in winter months. New ordinances prohibit discrimination on the basis of criminal history and mental illness, on top of federal anti-discrimination clauses. Tenants evicted for violating lease clauses and nonpayment have access to city-paid attorneys to fight eviction.

A growing number of condominiums in the association are now in foreclosure. The HOA is underfunded and unable to raise dues in the face of property owners' inability to recoup the higher dues through higher rents and longer periods of non-payment of rent from problem tenants. Sounds far-fetched? West Coast cities from Seattle to Los Angeles are implementing measures very similar.

Commercial real estate ownership is not a passive investment. Real estate prices are not guaranteed to increase. Property uses can be destroyed or severely limited. Investors cannot afford to be emotional or overly optimistic about properties. It is always better to cut one's losses short and preserve as much capital as possible for reinvestment. There is always another real estate opportunity as long as one retains the financial capacity to invest.

Chapter 9:
Selling Your Property

"You must never try to make all the money that's in a deal. Let the other fellow make some money too, because if you have a reputation for always making all the money, you won't have many deals."

J. Paul Getty

Launching your real estate portfolio with the purchase of a rental property or a home that can later be converted to a rental property or sold to provide capital for additional properties is the first half of your real estate decision. Eventually you need to successfully sell your property and either reinvest the proceeds or liquidate your ownership in the most tax-efficient manner possible. Knowing when you will need the equity you are building through real estate ownership helps make that process more efficient.

Considerations if Your Real Estate is Your Primary Residence

Until 1997, the IRS required homeowners to reinvest all profits from the sale of their home into another primary residence to avoid capital gains taxes. Sellers over age 55 could take a one-time $125,000 profit tax exemption, regardless of their use of the funds.

The Taxpayer Relief Act of 1997 changed the rules with the 121 Exclusion. Homeowners are now allowed to receive a Capital Gains Tax Exclusion of up to $250,000 ($500,000 if a married couple filling a joint return sells their home) without having any **federal,** and possibly state, capital gains tax liability as long as the house has been their primary residence for at least two of the past five years.

There is no limit on the number of times one may use the $250,000 (or $500,000) tax exemption, but it can only be used once every two years.

This tax benefit applies only to your primary residence. Second homes and rental properties do not qualify for this tax benefit.

Can you still take the Capital Gains Tax Exclusion if you convert your primary residence to a rental and later sell? Yes, but...

1. You cannot have taken the capital gains exclusion on another property in the last two-year period.

2. You must have lived in the house at least two of the prior five years.

121 Exclusion Can Be Combined With a §1031 Exchange

What if the gain on your home exceeds the tax exclusion amounts? Revenue Procedure 2005-14, issued and made effective on January 27, 2005, made it possible for the first time for homeowners to use the tax-deferral mechanism of Section §1031 on their primary residence, if done in conjunction with the specific strategy delineated under the Revenue Procedure.

Chapter 8 is dedicated to a discussion of Section §1031 and how it can be used to defer taxes. This is a very important tool for real estate investors, so take the time to read the chapter carefully and then consult with a §1031 professional before selling your existing property.

So long as the property in question satisfies the requirements for both Code Sections §1031 and 121, then the Section 121 Exclusion operates to exclude from taxable income either $250,000 (single or married filing separately) or $500,000 (married couple) in capital gain from the sale, exchange or disposition of the property. Any additional gain may be deferred by reinvesting in a like-kind replacement property through a tax-deferred §1031 exchange.

If Your Real Estate Has Not Been Your Primary Residence

Before you sell an investment property, talk with your tax professional to make certain you understand the tax implications of selling. Laws may have changed in the interval and your use of the property to produce income could impact your tax status. If, once your home was converted to a rental, you depreciated its value, definitely consult with a tax professional. Reg. Section 1.121-1(d) provides that the capital gains exclusion is not available against any previously claimed depreciation deductions against the residence.

If you originally purchased and have used the property as an investment property or do not meet the requirements for a primary residence capital gains exclusion, your options change.

- You can sell the property, pay taxes on gains and recaptured depreciation and invest your remaining funds in a new investment.

- You can defer taxes on gains and recaptured depreciation by using a §1031 exchange to reinvest in a new like-kind real estate investment(s).

If you intend to use a §1031 exchange, it is essential that you put the proper procedures in place BEFORE you sell. In our next chapter, we look at the §1031 exchange in more detail. But always talk with your tax adviser in advance to make certain you comply with IRS requirements. After the sale is too late.

The Sales Process

When it's time to sell your property and move on, your real estate team will assist you in developing a sales strategy to assure that your home sells at a high, competitive value based on its condition, unique selling features and market conditions.

But, first steps first. Let's look at the sales process and some of the decisions you need to make.

Should You Use a Real Estate Professional?

Before you decide to sell your property yourself and avoid paying a sales commission, you need to evaluate your ability and knowledge. Just as renting a property encounters an array of local state and federal laws, so does selling. Can you objectively set the right value for your property that optimizes your return, but doesn't leave the property sitting on the market of months waiting the right buyer?

There is also a definite skill in being able to work with buyers and buyers' real estate sales professionals, including the offer and counteroffer process. Your real estate professional will also help you escrow payments and put together a closing team.

A knowledgeable real estate agent or buyer's broker can guide you through the process of selling a property and make the process much easier. This assistance can be especially helpful to a seller with limited experience.

Before you select a Realtor, if you do not have a referral you trust to a good Realtor, make a point of interviewing three or four real estate professionals. If you have questions as to whether your property has greater value as a primary residence or an income producing property make certain and talk to a commercial real estate broker as well. The markets for residential and commercial properties can be distinctly different, as is the ability of the Realtor to reach the right market. A commercial agent may be better able to help you present the property as a business proposition, demonstrating its income producing potential and focusing on trends that could influence its resale value as a commercial property.

If the residential market is more lucrative for your property, then a residential agent should be better at reaching individual buyers.

A good agent will help you set a fair and competitive selling price to increase your odds of a quick sale. An agent will interact with potential buyers to make certain they are qualified and deal with lookie-loos who have no intention of writing an offer.

An agent will also have more experience negotiating sales than you do, potentially helping you get more money than you could on your own. Further, if any problems crop up during the process—they will be there to handle them for you. Finally, agents are familiar with all the paperwork and pitfalls involved in real estate transactions and can help make sure the process goes smoothly.

To give you an idea of what you should expect from your real estate professional, the following page shows a Listing Management Checklist we use when listing a home for sale. If you decide you want to sell your property yourself, make certain you are prepared and able to execute these steps yourself for a successful sale. And make certain you can avoid letting your emotions interfere with your ability to sell your property.

synergy | LISTING MANAGEMENT
CHECKLIST

NAME & PROPERTY ADDRESS

PRE-LISTING

- [ ] Prepare valuation
- [ ] Preview other listings
- [ ] Call other listing agents and agents of recently sold listings
- [ ] Compare valuation with other agents in office for second opinion
- [ ] Prepare all the necessary agreements and disclosures
- [ ] Order preliminary title report

LISTING APPOINTMENT

- [ ] Discuss clients' goals
- [ ] Identify improvements at property
- [ ] Discuss pricing and timing strategy
- [ ] Decide if it is a good client/agent fit. Is this a win-win?
- [ ] Execute paperwork, disclosures, and client to-do list
- [ ] Enroll in a Home Warranty

POST LISTING

- [ ] Final review of valuation and new market activity
- [ ] Hire photographer or take pictures
- [ ] Hire staging company
- [ ] Video tour
- [ ] Measure interior of home
- [ ] Install yard sign
- [ ] Input all the data into the MLS database
- [ ] Scan and upload disclosures and contract preparation docs to MLS
- [ ] Update any other third party sites like Zillow.com
- [ ] Update company website and personal website
- [ ] Create property website
- [ ] Upload photos or videos to YouTube for SEO (Search Engine Optimization)
- [ ] Share on social media pages
- [ ] Advertise home on social media sites
- [ ] Schedule open house
- [ ] Prepare open house marketing materials
- [ ] Post open house on Zillow, Craigslist, or in local paper
- [ ] Prepare property brochures
- [ ] Create Just Listed postcards
- [ ] Promote listing to in-house brokers
- [ ] Promote listing to outside brokers
- [ ] Email market listing to database

- [ ] Monitor market changes, new listings/-sold listings
- [ ] Contact client regarding market changes
- [ ] Answer any questions or concerns from clients
- [ ] Field and answer questions from other agents and prospective buyers
- [ ] Show home to any prospective buyers who contact agent directly
- [ ] Receive offers from other agents
- [ ] Review and compare offers
- [ ] Contact buyer's lender and verify buyer's qualifications
- [ ] Negotiate and counsel client on offers
- [ ] Prepare and calculate estimated net sheets for clients
- [ ] Advise other prospective buyers of current offer
- [ ] Prepare counter offer if applicable
- [ ] Execute acceptable contract

LISTING APPOINTMENT

- [ ] Send contract to title company
- [ ] Update status in MLS and other databases
- [ ] Cancel or update open house status
- [ ] Upload contracts and executed disclosure for brokerage and state requirements
- [ ] Update calendar with all dates and deadlines
- [ ] Request or send HOA documents for buyers
- [ ] Handle inspection and appraisal requests
- [ ] Negotiate inspection and appraisal issues
- [ ] Review any title insurance issues
- [ ] Present any modifications, such as date changes, to clients
- [ ] Prepare and schedule closing
- [ ] Attend closing
- [ ] Facilitate utility transfer and new owner questions
- [ ] Execute any remaining documents
- [ ] Verify accuracy of all closing documents

LISTING APPOINTMENT

- [ ] Upload all documents for brokerage and file storage requirements
- [ ] Follow up with clients regarding move out and transfer of possession
- [ ] Follow up with other agent regarding move in and possession
- [ ] Follow up with clients one week after closing to see if there are other questions

Prepping Your Property to Sell

What improvements you make to the property to enhance its sales appeal will vary based on whether you are targeting a commercial or residential market. If you are positioning the property as an income producing opportunity, you may want to have tenants in place creating a definite income stream. If you are selling the property for a personal home, having the home empty and refreshed may help it sell better.

Because buyers look carefully for signs of routine maintenance, basic improvements that we would recommend regardless of your target market include:

- Patch holes and cracks in walls and ceilings
- Repaint dark or marred walls with a neutral paint
- Fix broken appliances
- Make certain the HVAC systems are working properly
- Repair leaking faucets
- Fix the roof if it leaks
- Replace rotten wood
- Replace broken window glass
- Get rid of any mold
- Clean the carpet or replace worn or stained carpet
- Clean the windows and make certain the property is well lit

Pay attention also to street appeal, which is the first impression buyers will have of your property.

Any problem with the property will be uncovered during the buyer's inspection, so there's no use hiding it. Fix the problem ahead of time; price the property below market value to account for the problem or list the property at a competitive price but offer the buyer a credit to fix the problem.

Plan Ahead if You Intend to Reinvest Your Sale Proceeds

If you are considering a §1031 Exchange, you need to be aware of some very specific requirements:

1. You cannot take possession of the proceeds of the sale. Those funds must be held in escrow by a qualified intermediary (QI) until used for the purchase of your new property.

2. Any cash received from the sale of your existing property — your net proceeds after you pay off debt and closing costs — needs to be reinvested in a new property to defer capital gains taxes. Any funds withdrawn from the transaction could potentially be taxable.

3. Not only do you need to reinvest all your cash, you must buy property with the same or greater amount of debt. If you get a debt reduction, the IRS considers that a benefit and it could also be taxable.

4. You have 45 days from the closing of your first property to identify a replacement property(ies).

5. You have 180 days from closing on your first property to close on the replacement property(ies). These are calendar days, not business days.

Walk Through – SELLER'S JOURNEY

The following is a process built and refined by Synergy to maximize value, minimize taxes, and to keep you in control.

1. **Meet with a professional**
   There's no commitment required on your part for the initial meeting. It will be educational and help you identify the next steps.

2. **Establish a price**

   Your agent will provide a market analysis, which will help you set an asking price. *STRATEGIC PRICING — As difficult as it may be, it's important to review the market analysis and consider your home price objectively.*

3. **Prepare your home**

   View your home through the eyes of a buyer and ask yourself what you'd expect. Your agent will offer some useful suggestions.

4. **List your home**

   When everything is in place, your agent will put your home on the open market. It is critical you make it as easy as possible for potential buyers to view your home. *SHOWINGS — Potential buyers may ask to see your home on short notice. It's best if you can accommodate these requests, you never want to miss a potential sale.*

5. **Offers and negotiations**

   If everything goes well, a buyer (and most often the agent who represents them) will present your agent an offer. *CHOOSING AN OPTION — Your agent will present the benefits and risks of each offer. You will have the opportunity to either accept or counter any offer based on its merits.*

6. **Under contract**

   At this point, you and the buyer have agreed to all the terms of the offer and both parties have signed the agreement. *INSPECTION — The buyer will usually perform an inspection of the home. They may even ask you to make certain repairs. Your agent will explain all of your options regarding inspection.*

7. **Final details**

   While under contract, the buyer will work with their mortgage provider to finalize the loan and perform other due diligence.

8. **Closing**

    This is the transfer of funds and ownership. Depending on when the buyer moves into the home you will need to be all packed up and ready to move.

Chapter 10:

§1031 Tax Free Exchanges

Internal Revenue Code Section §1031

"No gain or loss shall be recognized on the exchange of property held for productive use in a trade or business or for investment if such property is exchanged solely for property of like kind which is to be held either for productive use in a trade or business or for investment."

The §1031 Exchange is one of the last tax shelters allowed by the IRS. By exchanging an investment property for like-kind investment property, an investor is able to defer (not eliminate) the payment of capital gain taxes, health care taxes, state taxes, and the recapture of depreciation taxes.

The recognition of tax-deferred, like-kind exchange structures in the U.S. tax code goes back to the early 1920s, taking its current form with the 1954 Amendment to the Federal Tax Code. Section §1031 of the Internal Revenue Code established the present-day definition and description of a tax-deferred, like-kind exchange, laying the groundwork for the current §1031 exchange transaction.

The Tax Cuts and Jobs Act of 2017 left intact §1031 exchanges of real property but repealed §1031 exchanges for all other types of property that are not real property.

The key benefit of a §1031 exchange is that it allows you to reinvest funds from the sale of an investment property without losing buying power to taxes. Instead of paying taxes on gains, you are able to defer taxes and reinvest the full amount of your proceeds in a like-kind property. A §1031 is not a tax-free exchange. While there are ways in which taxes may never need to be paid on real estate capital gains, since one of those involves dying, it's better look at the transaction as a means of deferring taxes.

In the example below, we look at the net proceeds available for reinvestment by deferring taxes using a §1031.

A multi-family rental property is originally purchased for $650,000 and held for 15 years before being sold for $1,250,000. Straight line depreciation over 27.5 years is used, making the adjusted cost basis at the time of sale $295,454. It is assumed the seller is in the maximum tax bracket, triggering the net investment income tax.

	A	B
	Sells Property Pays Taxes	**Defers Taxes with §1031 Exchange**
Purchase price	$650,000	$650,000
Depreciation	$354,545	$354,545
Adjusted Cost Basis	$295,454	$295,454
Sale Price	$1,250,000	$1,250,000
Total Taxable Gain	$954,546	$954,546
Federal Long-term Capital Gain Liability (20% of $954,546)	$190,909	$0
State Tax	-?-	-?-
Net Investment Income Tax (3.8% of $954,546)	$36,273	$0
Depreciation Recapture Tax (25% of $354,545)	$88,636	$0
Total Taxes Due	$315,818	$0
NET PROCEEDS FOR RE-INVESTMENT	$934,182	$1,250,000

Understanding the §1031 Exchange

The IRS defines like-kind property as all real property held for investment purposes or the productive use in a trade or business. Short-term transactions, such as flipping properties, are not allowed.

Transactions Excluded from §1031 Exchanges:

1. Stock and trade or other property held primarily for sale

2. Personal property

3. Interest in a partnership
    - Considered personal property rather than interest in the underlying real estate

4. International exchanges
    - Prevents owners from exchanging overseas where the money never returns to the U.S.

5. Vacation homes that do not meet the IRS's personal use limit
    - Maximum of 14 days personal use per year or 10% of rental time, whichever is greater, during the first two-year period

6. Related party exchanges
    - Simultaneous exchange with a family member
    - Delayed exchange selling to a related party
    - Delayed exchange purchasing from a related party

§1031 Requirements

1. 1031 exchanges require re-investment of all sale proceeds or payment of taxes on money not reinvested. Reinvestment can be in multiple properties.

2. Properties must meet the **like-kind requirement** — properties held for productive use in a trade or business or held for investment and not for resale purposes — no short-term transactions.

3. Same or greater amount of debt must be maintained — there can be no debt reduction.

4. Proceeds for original sale are held in an escrow account by qualified intermediary.

5. Within 45 days of sale up to three replacement properties must be identified in writing or an unlimited number of properties may be identified provided that the fair market value of all the properties does not exceed 200% of the fair market value of the relinquished property. This gives the investor options in the event a preferred property cannot be purchased.

6. The exchange must be completed within 180 days (or the day your tax return is due).

The taxpayer that owns the Original Property must be the one that takes title to the New Property and reports the §1031 exchange on its tax return. If the original property is owned by a Limited Liability Corporation (LLC), or a Limited Partnership (LP), the new property must be held by the same entity or the exchange will be disallowed. If a commercial property is held by a legal partnership or LLC, all partners must agree to roll over the sale proceeds through an exchange or cash out. One partner cannot cash out while the others continue to hold their shares.

If title is held as tenants-in-common, with each investor filing a separate tax return, individual investors can decide whether or not they want to take their proceeds from the sale and pay taxes without the concurrence of the other owners.

Types of §1031 Exchanges

1031 Exchanges may be *simultaneous* or *delayed*. In both cases, no cash proceeds from the transaction can be held by the seller.

In a *simultaneous* exchange, the parties simply exchange deeds.

The more usual form of exchange is the *delayed* exchange in which the sale proceeds from the original property are held by the exchange intermediary or exchange facilitator and paid directly to the seller of the new property. If at any point the original seller has possession of the sale proceeds, the transaction is disqualified from §1031 benefits.

The delayed exchange allows for the sale of the original property, followed by an offer and closing on the replacement property(ies). At the closing for the replacement property, the exchange intermediary transfers the funds held from the original sale to the seller of the replacement property. At this point, the original property owner has the option of cashing out a portion of the sale proceeds. However, those proceeds immediately become liable for capital gains and depreciation recovery taxes.

Reverse §1031 Exchanges

What if the owner of the original property decides to sell because a more desirable property has come on the market? Waiting until the original property sells could mean losing the opportunity to purchase the desired property. A *"reverse exchange,"* in which the replacement property is purchased before the original property is sold, is also possible.

In this situation, the owner of the original property buys the new property and transfers legal title to an Exchange Accommodations Titleholder (EAT). The purchaser cannot take title to the replacement property outright if it is to qualify for an exchange. It must be "parked" first until the property to be relinquished is sold. Once that property is sold, title to the new property can be regained using the sale proceeds and taxes will be deferred on gains acquired by the sale.

The EAT has to convey title back to the purchaser no later than 180 days after acquiring it. While the EAT holds the title to the property, the purchaser is required to manage and care for the property and is entitled to the net profits from rental income during the holding period.

If you may be in a situation where you need to use a reverse exchange, make certain you review the IRS revenue procedures explain the "parking" guidelines relating to a reverse §1031 exchange.

Non-Safe Harbor Exchanges

What if you do a reverse exchange, and are then unable to sell your original property within 180 days? Under Revenue Procedure 2037 you can only park a property with an EAT for 180 days. If you are outside the safe harbor of 180 days, you need to make very certain the EAT that's holding title to the replacement property cannot be deemed to be an agent of the taxpayer i.e. you as the entity trying to make the 1031 exchange.

If you are in this situation, make certain you have your own separate legal and tax advisor working with you throughout the entire process and that you are parking your property with a qualified intermediary. If you do not meet §1031 rules, your exchange can be disqualified and taxable.

The Like-kind Requirement

The like-kind requirement is integral to a §1031 exchange. A like-kind property is real estate held for investment purposes or for use in a trade or business. It is not necessary to exchange into the same use such as retail or residential. The key criterion is that the property be held for investment. One **cannot** exchange:

- from a personal residence into investment property
- from an investment property into a residence
- from real estate located within the U.S. to real estate located abroad
- from ownership of an entity which owns real estate (such as an LLC or a general or limited partnership) into another such entity; or
- from direct, titled ownership into an entity which owns real estate or vice versa

From One to Multiple Properties

It is possible to exchange one property for multiple properties. Suppose you own a residential rental property now worth $800,000. Using the "200% rule" you can identify any number of replacement properties *provided that the aggregate value of all property on the identification list does not exceed 200% of the value of the relinquished property.* Since the relinquished property is worth $800,000, the aggregate value of identified properties cannot exceed $1,600,000. That gives the exchanger the ability to have "fall-back" properties in the event target properties cannot be acquired within the 180 days.

Under the Treasury Regulations, the basis from the original property must be allocated among the multiple replacement properties in proportion to their respective values.

A multiple property exchange allows:

- 100% tax deferral on the sale of the relinquished property
- Potentially increased cash flow through multiple properties
- Less reliance on one tenant for income
- Diversification into different real estate markets
- Increased flexibility — one of the newly acquired properties could be sold to generate cash while recognizing gain on only a proportion of the original investment

Exchanging into Fractional Ownership

As many real estate owners age, they run into a common problem of wanting to eliminate active management of their properties, but not wanting to cash out and incur substantial taxes or experience the loss of steady income from their real estate holdings. Real estate investors may also want to "trade-up" to acquire ownership of larger or more expensive properties where they share risks and obligations with others.

March 2002, the IRS issued Revenue Rule 2002-22, which allows a property owner to "trade up" into a "fractional interest" in a larger property with multiple owners.

Ownership by multiple parties typically facilitates larger investments such as multiple-unit apartment complexes, retail centers, large office buildings, etc. In selecting the right investment structure, it is important to look at how decisions are made and the how interests of the individual investors are protected. In collective ownership structures, unanimous, or even majority approval of the investors can be a challenge.

Prohibited Ownership Structures

The typical way multiple ownership of a property is achieved is through a Limited Liability Corporation (LLC) or Limited Partnership (LP), but these ownership forms are considered stock ownership and prohibited from use in a §1031 exchange. (Although an LLC or LP can sell properties within its portfolio and exchange them for like-kind properties where title is taken in the name of the partnership or LLC.)

Permitted Ownership Structures

An early use of Revenue Rule 2002-22 in §1031 exchanges was the Tenant-in-Common or TIC exchange. While the concept was good, implementation of TIC ownership ran into some problems resulting in a black eye for the industry.

Delaware Statutory Trusts (DSTs) have largely replaced the TIC as a tool for partial ownership and are discussed later in this book.

§1031 Exchanges Combined With 121 Exclusion

The 121 Exclusion is the ability of single people or married couples filing separately to exclude from taxes up to $250,000 per person in capital gains from the sale of their residence on their federal tax returns. Married couples filing jointly have an exclusion limit of

$500,000. No capital gains taxes are owed on profit from the sale of a home until it exceeds the exclusion.

But what if the homeowners meet the requirements for a 121 exclusion but convert the property to a rental? Have they lost their ability to exclude capital gains from taxes?

The IRS issued and made effective Revenue Procedure 2005-14 on January 27, 2005, making it possible for the first time for homeowners to take advantage of the 121 exclusion and use the tax-deferral mechanism of Section §1031 on the residence, if done in conjunction with the specific strategy delineated under the Revenue Procedure.

So long as the property in question satisfies the requirements for both Code Sections §1031 and 121 (the property was the primary home of the sellers for two of the preceding five years), then the Section 121 Exclusion operates to exclude from taxable income either $250,000 or $500,000 in capital gain from the sale, exchange or disposition of the property. Any additional gain may be deferred by reinvesting in like-kind replacement property through a tax-deferred like-kind exchange.

It is best to obtain legal advice to make certain you are following the IRS's required steps to assure that your transaction is compliant with Revenue Procedure 2005-14.

What if you have a rental property that you convert to your primary residence? Can you sell the property and use the 121 exclusion once you have lived in it for two of the last five years?

Yes, but...to prevent people from abusing the exclusion to eliminate taxes on rental properties, some rules were added effective in 2009 imposing some limitations on the use of 121. First, the seller will owe tax on the "recapture" of depreciation taken during the rental years. Second, capital gains attributable to the number of years the property was a rental after Jan. 1, 2009 are taxable. This can become relatively complex, so work with your tax adviser before selling.

Useful Applications for a §1031 Exchange

A §1031 exchange is a means of solving problems and taking advantage of new opportunities.

Leverage Existing Equity into a Better Property or Multiple Properties

Many individuals, particularly those who transitioned a former residence into an investment property, have a property that is fully paid off, fully depreciated and tying up a lot of equity. If they sell the property and cash out, they could easily be paying capital gains taxes in excess of 23% and depreciation recapture taxes of 25%.

By selling the property and utilizing a §1031 exchange, they are able to defer taxes and all of their proceeds are available to invest in one or more replacement properties. They can leverage their investment through new debt, regaining interest and depreciation deductions and potentially increasing cash flow even after mortgage payments. And they are back to benefiting from appreciation on the portion of the property funded through new debt.

Diversify the Real Estate Portfolio

An investor might own several single-family rental homes accumulated over years of investing. With a §1031 exchange, the individual can diversify by investing in different geographic markets, different price brackets, or even different real estate uses, such office buildings or commercial properties.

Consolidate Real Estate Holdings

Perhaps instead of multiple single-family residences you would like to own a single apartment or office building where economies of scale could be implemented to improve cash flow.

Improve Cash Flow

Maybe you have invested in vacant land, or low-rent residential properties that require considerable maintenance. By selling the property and using a §1031 Exchange, all of your transaction proceeds are available to invest in a property or properties that will produce better cash flow. By leveraging up to more expensive real estate, depreciation write-offs will also come back into play.

Improve Appreciation Potential

You may want to dispose of property in a slow market area and acquire property in a market with great demand and higher appreciation rates.

Exploit Opportunities in the Market

Economic developments and new planned uses of surrounding properties may create a short-term mark up in real estate values. The designation of **Opportunity Zones** to spur economic development by providing tax benefits to investors, for example, created a demand for properties in the newly designated zones. While existing owners are not able to benefit from the tax incentives, they can benefit from higher prices as investors look for areas to invest.

Eliminate Personal Management

Many investment property owners are also the property managers and may be ready to get rid of the headaches of maintenance and tenants, but still want the cash flow and benefits of real estate ownership.

There are a number of ways to eliminate active management and still benefit from owning real estate. With triple-net leased commercial properties, the tenant is responsible for upkeep, maintenance, taxes, insurance, etc. Partial ownership of professionally managed properties through one of today's most popular instruments, the Delaware Statutory Trust, is another option.

Divide Real Estate Without Incurring Taxes

Maybe you purchased an apartment building with your brother-in-law, who is moving to a new state and would rather own property in that state. You could sell the existing building and purchase two new properties in different locations.

This can also work with estate planning where parents may want to divide their real estate holdings among their three children in such a manner that there are no disputes after their death. Using a §1031 exchange, they could roll their equity over into three separate properties, chosen by their children. The properties would then pass to the designated individual on their death (and yes, this is one way in which capital gains taxes may never be paid because the properties are marked to market when inherited).

Acquire Property for Future Conversion to Personal Use

It is also possible to use a §1031 exchange to acquire property that you want to convert to your personal residence or vacation home in the future. While this is possible, it is also subject to a number of rules that need to be followed to avoid having the exchange disqualified.

Internal Revenue Code Section 1031 Summary

"No gain or loss shall be recognized on the exchange of property held for productive use in a trade or business or for investment if such property is exchanged solely for property of like kind which is to be held either for productive use in a trade or business or for investment."

Key Rules

- **Like-kind requirement** — properties held for productive use in a trade or business or held for investment and not for resale purposes

- **Same or greater amount of debt maintained** — no debt reduction
- **Proceeds from original sale held in an escrow** account by qualified intermediary
- **Three ways to identify replacement properties within 45 days of sale of the investment property:**
    - **Three property rule**
      Up to three replacement properties identified in writing. One, two or all three of the properties may be acquired in the exchange.

    - **200% rule**
      An unlimited number of properties may be identified provided that the fair market value of all the properties does not exceed 200% of the fair market value of the relinquished property.

    - **95% rule**
      More than three properties with a total value that is more than 200% of the value of the relinquished property can be identified, but only if at least 95% of the value of the properties that are identified are acquired.

- **180 days to complete the transaction** (or the day your tax return is due if sooner). If there is more than one relinquished property in one exchange, the 45 days are measured from the date the first relinquished property closes.

Reasons to Sell Property Via a 1031 Exchange

- Leverage — Great way to buy more real estate and/or achieve greater cash flow
- Higher tax basis — Lower rates
- Diversification — 1 building for 2 or more, location and/or type
- Taxes — Defer them
- Consolidation — Many properties into one (more doors)

- Increased Depreciation — Buy bigger
- Management Relief — Mailbox money and no more tenants, toilets, and trash
- Estate Planning — Land to apartment — Transition for no cash flow to a cash flow property — 3 kids doing different things, sell ranch and diversify into 3 properties selected by each child

1031 Terminology

Basis: Original cost, plus improvements, minus depreciation taken.

Boot: Fair Market Value of non-qualified property (i.e., property that is not of "like kind") received in an exchange. (Examples: cash, notes, seller financing, furniture, supplies, reduction in debt obligations). Taxable to the extent there is capital gain.

Cash Boot: Any proceeds actually or constructively received by the taxpayer.

Constructive Receipt: Although an investor does not have actual possession of the proceeds, he or she is legally entitled to the proceeds in some manner such as having the money held by an entity considered as his or her agent or by someone having a fiduciary relationship with him or her. This creates a taxable event.

Direct Deeding: Transfer of title directly from the taxpayer to buyer and from the seller to taxpayer after all necessary exchange documents have been executed.

Exchanger: The property owner(s) seeking to defer capital gain tax by utilizing a Section 1031 exchange. (The Internal Revenue Code uses the term "taxpayer."

Exchange Agreement: The written agreement defining the transfer of the relinquished property, the subsequent receipt of the replacement property, and the restrictions on the exchange proceeds during the exchange period.

Exchange Period: The period of time in which replacement property must be received by the taxpayer; ends on the earlier of 180 calendar days after the relinquished property closing or the due date for the taxpayer's tax return (If the 180th day falls after the due date of the taxpayer's tax return, an extension may be filed to receive the full 180-day exchange period).

Identification Period: A maximum of 45 calendar days from the relinquished property closing to identify potential replacement property(ies).

Like-kind Property: Any property held for productive use in trade or business or held for investment; both the relinquished and replacement properties must be considered like-kind to qualify for tax deferral.

Mortgage Boot: This occurs when the taxpayer does not acquire debt that is equal to or greater than the debt that was paid off on the relinquished property sale; referred to as debt relief. This creates a taxable event.

Qualified Intermediary: The person or entity that facilitates the exchange for the Exchanger. The term "facilitator" or "accommodator" is also commonly used, although Treasury Regulations use the term "Qualified Intermediary."

Relinquished Property: The property "sold" by the Exchanger. This is also sometimes referred to as the "exchange" property or the "downleg" property.

Replacement Property: The property "acquired" by the Exchanger. Sometimes referred to as the "acquisition" property or the "upleg" property.

Taxable Gain: Selling price minus Basis.

Chapter 11:
Passive Real Estate Investments

"Current real estate prices aren't high because they have been driven up by irresponsible speculation. As was often the case in the past. Prices have risen because a constantly increasing population with money to invest has been created — and continues to be created."

J. Paul Getty

There is a wide spectrum of investment opportunities when it comes to owning real estate. You can choose to be a passive investor, a partial owner or an active investor, selecting and owning your own properties. To select the right investment structure, start by sitting down with your investment team to:

1. **Clearly identify your investment objectives and constraints.**

   - Do you want income producing property or speculative property?
   - Do you want a diversified real estate portfolio or a focused portfolio?
   - Given the characteristics of available types of properties — single family, multi-family, retail, office, warehouse, raw land, agricultural land, etc. — which type better meets your investment goals?
   - What are your financial and non-financial constraints? *Often this financial goal is stated in terms of discounted cash flows (net present value) or an internal rate of return (IRR).*
   - How much money do you want to allocate to the real estate portion of your portfolio?

- Do you require positive cash flow?
- What is your holding period?

2. **Establish how you will fund the investment.**

- What is the source of your purchase funds?
- Will you use debt financing?
- Will rental income be sufficient to meet loan costs?
- Will you use funds in your IRA?
- If you are selling an existing property, are you using a §1031 exchange?

3. **Determine the level of control you want over your investment.**

Investment Objectives & Constraints

- Do you want to own and manage the investment directly?
- Do you want partial ownership with or without management responsibilities?
- How important is liquidity?

Funding

Level of Control

Real estate investments can be made through an (1) indirect purchase of real estate such as Real Estate Investment Trusts (REITs); mutual

Investment Vehicle

funds and Exchange Traded Funds (ETFs) that invest in both publicly traded and privately traded REITS; (2) partial ownership through investment vehicles such as Limited Partnerships (LP), Limited Liability Corporations (LLC) and Delaware Statutory Trusts (DST) or (3) through a direct purchase of property in which you may choose to improve the property for resale or use it as a commercial or residential rental.

Partial ownership through LP, LLC, and DST structures typically require the investor to be "accredited," indicating a higher level of sophistication and knowledge of investing. To qualify as an accredited investor as of 2019, at least one of the following requirements must be met:

1.   Have a net worth exceeding $1 million individually or combined with a spouse (excluding value of primary residence).

2.   Have earned income exceeding $200,000 ($300,000 if combined with a spouse) during each of the last two calendar years and demonstrate credibility he or she will at least maintain these income thresholds during the current year.

If you are just starting out in your investment career and have limited income and net worth, your options may be limited to investments that do not require you to be an accredited investor.

Crowdfunding is also maturing as a means for non-accredited investors to participate in private equity investments. But this is still an industry in transition with considerable risks for the inexperienced investor.

Real Estate Investment Trusts

For individuals just starting to build the real estate portion of their investment portfolio, REITs are a low involvement, relatively low entry cost investment opportunity.

REIT stands for Real Estate Investment Trust. A REIT typically comes in one of two structures — publicly traded or privately-traded.

The majority of REITs are publicly traded on either the New York Stock Exchange (NYSE) or the NASDAQ. Units in a publicly traded REIT are purchased much as one would buy individual securities or stocks issued by publicly traded companies. Publicly traded REITs have the advantage of being very liquid and transparent. In addition to knowing what they own, investors can analyze the REIT's track records.

Privately traded REITs lack the liquidity and transparency of publicly traded REITS and as a result are available only to qualified investors. Private REITs are sold through both securities brokers and investment advisors, with different compensation plans. A securities broker/ dealer typically charges an up-front commission reducing the amount invested in the REIT. The compensation structure for an investment advisor is typically fee based on assets under management resulting in the full amount actually invested in the REIT.

REITs were established by Congress in the 1960s to enable the general public to invest in real estate and directly participate in the higher returns that can be produced through commercial real estate ownership — without actually having to go out and buy commercial real estate. Each unit in a REIT represents a proportionate fraction of ownership in each of the underlying properties.

REITs historically have delivered competitive total returns, based on steady dividend income and long-term capital appreciation. Their comparatively low correlation with other asset classes can help reduce overall portfolio risk and increase returns.

The advantage of the REIT structure is that REITs are generally exempt from taxation at the trust level as long they distribute at least 90% of their income to their unitholders. Instead of passing through after-tax profits, they pass cash flow directly to unitholders. Corporate taxation is paid only on retained income.

Dividend payments made by the REIT are taxed to the unitholder as ordinary income, unless they are considered qualified dividends, which are taxed as capital gains. Otherwise, the dividend is taxed at the unitholder's top marginal tax rate.

For a company to qualify as a REIT, it must meet several qualifications:

- Be an entity that would be taxable as a corporation but for its REIT status
- Be managed by a board of directors or trustees
- Have shares that are fully transferable

- Have a minimum of 100 shareholders after its first year as a REIT
- Have no more than 50% of its shares held by five or fewer individuals during the last half of the taxable year
- Invest at least 75% of its total assets in real estate assets and cash
- Derive at least 75% of its gross income from real estate related sources, including rents from real property and interest on mortgages financing real property
- Derive at least 95% of its gross income from such real estate sources and dividends or interest from any source
- Have no more than 25% of its assets consist of non-qualifying securities or stock in taxable REIT subsidiaries

REITs generally fall into three categories: equity REITs that own real estate, mortgage REITs that finance real estate, and hybrid REITs, which invest in both equity properties and mortgage securities. For this discussion, we are only looking at equity REITs that invest in commercial real estate. These REITs operate along a straight-forward and easily understandable business model: By leasing space and collecting rent on its real estate, the company generates income, which is then paid out to shareholders in the form of dividends.

Equity REIT Investment Categories

Most equity REITS specialize in specific real estate markets, allowing investors to choose property types in which they would like to invest. Real estate investments generally fall in the following classes:

- **Office REITs** own and manage office real estate, renting space in those properties to tenants. They may focus on central business districts, suburban areas, or specific classes of tenants, such as government agencies or biotech firms.
- **Retail REITs** own and manage retail real estate and rent space in those properties to tenants. They may specialize in large regional malls, outlet centers, grocery-anchored shopping

centers, centers with big box retailers or free-standing retail stores.

- **Industrial REITs** own and manage industrial facilities such as warehouses and distribution centers and rent space in those properties to tenants.

- **Net lease REITs** structure their leases so that tenants pay both rent and the majority of operating expenses for a property, resulting in relatively little management involvement by the REIT.

- **Lodging REITs** own and manage hotels and resorts and rent space to guests.

- **Residential REITs** own and manage various forms of residences, leasing space in those properties to tenants. They may focus on apartment buildings, student housing, single-family homes, manufactured homes, specific geographical markets or classes of properties such as class A, B or C apartment buildings.

- **Timberland REITs** own and manage timberland real estate, specializing in harvesting and selling timber.

- **Health care REITs** own and manage health care-related real estate and collect rent from tenants. This may include senior living facilities, hospitals, medical office buildings, skilled nursing facilities and other health-care related properties.

- **Self-storage REITs** own and manage storage facilities, collecting rent from storage customers.

- **Infrastructure REITs** own and manage infrastructure real estate such as fiber cables, telecommunications towers, wireless infrastructure, and energy pipelines.

- **Data center REITs** own and manage facilities used to safely store data, offering uninterruptable power supplies, air-cooled chillers and physical security.

- **Diversified REITs** own and manage a catch-all of property types and collect rent from tenants.

- **Specialty REITs** own and manage a unique mix of property types that might include movie theaters, casinos, farmland and outdoor advertising sites, collecting rent from tenants.

REITs are structured primarily total return investments. In addition to steady dividends, they tend to provide long-term returns competitive with those of stocks, as well as:

- **Liquidity** — Publicly listed REITs are readily traded on the major stock exchanges.

- **Transparency** — REITs are required to abide by the rules and regulations of the Securities Exchange Commission. Independent directors, analysts and auditors, as well as the business and financial media monitor listed REITs' performances and outlook.

- **Low capital requirements** to achieve a diversified portfolio of real estate investments.

Investing in REIT Mutual Funds and ETFs

Ideally, you want to invest in REITs that own great properties and have great tenants. If you are not comfortable with your ability to select and monitor individual REITs, there are mutual funds and ETFs that are happy to take on the job for you. While these investment structures add another layer of costs, they also add a layer of expert management.

The primary difference between mutual funds and ETFs is the way they trade. A mutual fund is priced based on the NAV or net asset value of its holdings at the close of the market. If you put in an order to purchase shares of a mutual fund, that order is executed based on the closing price of the day you make a purchase. ETFs are Exchange Traded Funds and are priced as of their current trading value at the time you place an order, similar to stocks. If you purchase an **Index** mutual fund or ETF, the fund will hold positions designed to mimic the performance of a published index, often holding the same equities and weighting as the index.

As with any investment, there are risks to investing in both REITs and real estate mutual funds. Returns are not guaranteed. Real estate tends to go through market cycles as well as geographic cycles. When real estate markets falter, so will REITs and funds with REIT investments in geographic regions or market sectors. Real estate is also very vulnerable to rising interest rates, loss in the desirability of a location, natural disasters, bankruptcy of a major tenant, and specific property issues. As with any investment there is always the potential for loss as well as profit.

Chapter 12:
Purchasing Partial Ownership

"It is better to not do any real estate deals at all than to get yourself into a bad one. Bad deals will cost you money, time, and your sanity—and perhaps your business, friends, and family."

Kevin Perk

The first part of this book largely dealt with building an income producing real estate portfolio starting with residential rentals. This tactic allows you to build a portfolio with relatively modest initial money but involves considerable investment of your personal time. While single-owner real estate investments have provided exceptional returns over the years for many individuals, as time passes three problems typically arise:

- Cash flow requirements increase as the property owners retire
- Capital gains taxes diminish the appeal of selling properties to enjoy the equity built up in the properties
- The maintenance burden becomes difficult for the owner to manage

Several opportunities exist to purchase a partial interest in a larger income-producing property where there is less personal involvement but many comparable benefits.

Some of these investments are limited to "Qualified" or "Accredited" investors. A qualified or accredited investor is defined in the Securities Act of 1993, Regulation D as meeting certain criteria, such as exceeding an annual income or net worth level. These individuals are deemed to have sufficient financial sophistication to be excluded from certain U.S. regulations that are designed to protect investors.

For example, companies that wish to raise capital from individuals without issuing registered securities must limit their search to accredited investors.

As of 2021, accredited investors can include natural persons who:

- Have a net worth exceeding $1 million individually or combined with spouse (excluding value of primary residence);

- Have earned income exceeding $200,000 ($300,000 is combined with spouse) during each of the last two calendar years and demonstrate credibility that he or she will at least maintain these income thresholds during the current year;

- Maintain certain professional qualifications in good standing, including the Series 7, 65, and 82;

- Are "knowledgeable employees" (as defined under the Investment Company Act of 1940, as amended) of the issuing private fund, including executive officers, directors, and certain employees of the private fund or its affiliated manager; or

- Are "family clients" of a family office, as that term is defined under the Investment Advisers Act of 1940, as amended.

New opportunities are opening up for non-accredited investors to participate in partial ownership through crowdfunding. The 2012 Jumpstart Our Business Startups Act (JOBS) was passed to make it easier for small businesses to raise capital and, in turn, spur economic growth through job creation. Title III of the act deals specifically with crowdfunding.

In October 2015, the U.S. Securities and Exchange Commission (SEC) finalized some key provisions permitting non-accredited investors to participate in crowdfunded investments. As a result, new opportunities have opened up for non-accredited individuals to participate in partial ownership of real estate. The risks associated with crowdfunding can be quite a bit higher than investing in more established companies, however, and individuals venturing into these markets need to understand the risks of investing as well as the opportunity the investment may present.

Options for Partial Ownership

Partial ownership of investment real estate typically falls in the following ownership classes:

- Real estate investment trusts (REITs)
- Real estate exchange traded funds (ETFs)
- Commingled real estate funds (CREFs)
- Infrastructure funds
- Tenants in Common (TICs)
- Limited Partnerships (LP)
- Limited Liability Corporations (LLC)
- Delaware Statutory Trusts (DST)

For a discussion of REITs and real estate ETFs, refer back Chapter 2.

Commingled and Infrastructure Funds

A *commingled fund* is a single fund or account made up of assets from multiple accounts that have been "commingled" or "pooled" into one account for the purchase of properties. Although a commingled fund is registered with the SEC, it is not publicly listed or available to individual retail investors. Instead, it usually features in retirement plans, pension funds, insurance policies, and other institutional accounts. Because commingled funds do not have to comply with mutual fund regulations, they are typically lower cost to operate.

Infrastructure funds invest more than 60% of their assets in stocks of companies engaged in activities considered to be part of the infrastructure sector. These include oil and gas midstream; waste management; airports; integrated shipping; railroads; shipping and ports; trucking; engineering and construction; infrastructure operations; the utilities sector, etc.

Tenancy-In-Common (TIC) Ownership

Tenancy-in-common is a form of concurrent ownership in which two or more persons each have an undivided interest in the entire property, but no right of survivorship. When a tenant in common dies, the property passes to that tenant's estate.

Each independent owner may control equal or different percentages of the total property, but no individual may claim ownership to any specific part of the property. Because each person's interest, or share, is undivided, each can sell his share at any time without the consent or agreement of the others.

Contract terms for tenants in common are detailed in the deed, title, or other legally binding property ownership documents.

TIC ownership can offer advantages over traditional real estate partnerships, where limited partners give up their rights and much of their profits to the General Partner. But they can also encounter management issues when there is no clear decision maker. Operational costs can be problematic if one tenant encounters financial difficulty. In many jurisdictions, each owner may be liable for the property tax up to the full amount of the assessment regardless of their share of ownership. Because an individual tenant can sell his or her share of ownership, new joint tenants can be added to the agreement without the concurrence of the other owners.

While TIC ownership is a long-standing legal concept, Revenue Ruling 2002-22 opened §1031 exchanges up to this form of ownership by establishing rules for exchanging a single-owner property to a multi-owner property in the form of Tenants in Common (TIC). This allowed a property owner to "trade up" into partial ownership of a larger commercial enterprise. The original owner gains a "fractional interest" in the larger property where economies of scale can work to his advantage.

In permitting the use of TICs for §1031 exchanges, the IRS set specific requirements:

- There must be 35 or fewer co-owners.
- Unanimous co-owner approval is required for sale, refinancing, leasing, and management hiring; majority co-owner approval is required for other group actions.
- Although co-owners may hire a manager (who may be the sponsor) to operate the property, the manager can be compensated only based on the gross rental income, not based on profits or investor return, and the owners retain final decision-making authority.
- Each co-owner must retain the right to borrow against or transfer his/her share, or to partition the property (meaning force sale with proceeds allocated pro rata).
- Co-owners must share pro rata (by titled ownership percentage) all income, expenses, debt service, profits and cash distributions, and a no one who is not on title (such as the sponsor) may share in these amounts.
- The sponsor, broker, or syndicator may be paid reasonable compensation based on the fair market value of the property but may not be paid based on profits or investor return.

If any of these rights are given up or limited under the TIC agreement, then the TIC will probably not satisfy §1031 exchange requirements, and the investor is likely to face back taxes, penalties and interest if he/she is audited.

Although, owners may have different percentages of ownership, they all have equal rights to the property. No single owner can claim to own any certain part of the property; force other owners to contribute towards improvements made without consent; lease any part of the property without having to account to co-owners for rent received; or sell the entire property without the others' consent.

Under the Rev. Proc. 2002-22 like-kind tax deferred exchange requirements listed above, a person doing a §1031 exchange into a TIC must be named on the title to the property being acquired and must be listed as a borrower on any mortgage.

This puts investors at considerable risk. Each tenant in common could be held personally responsible for the full amount of the mortgage, as well as for any debt or loss resulting from environmental contamination, personal injury, or any other property-related problem. Liability insurance can't protect against losses that exceed policy limits or uninsured losses, such as earthquake or flood damage.

The unanimous approval control structure of TICs turned out to be the industry's Achilles heel in the recession of 2005 to 2009 and accompanying real estate market crash. Many 1031 TIC exchanges went into foreclosure because TIC members were unable to agree on the steps they needed to take to counter the loss of tenants and fall in commercial real estate values. While TICs still exist, lenders are now very hesitant to lend under a TIC investment property structure.

Limited Liability Companies (LLC)

The limited liability company is another option for purchasing partial ownership in a commercial property. I am going to skip the long version of what an LLC is and leave that to your attorney, but, briefly defined, an LLC is a form of business entity that provides limited liability protection, passthrough tax treatment of profits and losses, and the ability to transfer property in and out of an LLC with minimal tax consequences.

Using an LLC is similar to investing in a real estate investment trust (REIT) in that your funds are invested in limited interests, which are somewhat similar to investing in shares of a company's stock. The difference here is that LLCs are private, and there are usually only a few investors that are limited members and a developer that is the managing member.

A drawback of LLC ownership can be a lack of liquidity. When investing, it is critical to have a disposition time frame or means of liquidating one's position in the LLC at some point. Single-property limited liability corporations, for example, give investors the opportunity to acquire ownership in specific properties with an established disposition time frame at which point the property will be sold and proceeds distributed to investors, providing planned liquidity.

ONE WAY AN LLC MAY BE USED

You know a developer who is getting ready to start a new project in your local area. He has used $1,000,000 of his own money to purchase the land and now is trying to raise capital to develop the property. Once the project is finished and the condos are sold, he expects to realize a large profit. He is willing to give up some of his profit in exchange for the needed capital.

The name of his company is ABC Construction Company, LLC. After your attorney has reviewed the proper agreements and you have done your due diligence, you may decide to purchase the units of ABC Construction Company, LLC that have been agreed upon with the developer.

Depending upon your agreement, you recapture your investment and any gains as the units are sold. Because you hold what is essentially stock in the LLC, you cannot use a §1031 exchange to defer taxes and reinvest those funds in another real estate property.

A key disadvantage of LLC ownership can be a lack of liquidity. If the investor needs access to his funds prior to disposition of the property, there may not be an efficient means of cashing out.

Limited Partnerships (LP)

Limited Partnerships are often a preferred vehicle to meet the income tax requirements of international investors. Management of a limited partnership rests with the "general partner," who also bears unlimited liability for the company's debt and obligations. An experienced property manager or real estate development firm typically serves as the general partner. A limited partnership can include any number of "limited partners," whose liability is limited to the total amount of their investment in the company. Business profit and loss are "passed through" to the partners for reporting on their personal tax returns.

Single-property LPs provide investors with greater discretion over their investment. These business forms are established to own a specific property, providing investment transparency as well as the ability to conduct independent due diligence on the property prior to investment. As with single-property LLCs, these LP investments are marketed with an established disposition plan, giving the investor a liquidity timetable. Single-property LPs also help to ensure that liability against one property is self-contained.

LPs can also hold multiple properties and buy and sell properties within into portfolio. As long as the title is held in the same manner, these transactions may qualify for §1031 exchanges. Similar to LLCs, however, proceeds from the LLC cannot be used for a §1031 exchange. A critical drawback of the LP ownership form can be a lack of liquidity should an investor need to terminate an investment prior to sale and disposition.

The caution needs to be made with respect to disposition plans that real estate markets are uncertain and there can be no guarantee that the property will show a profit at the targeted disposition timeframe. Investors may find themselves holding on to a property longer than intended to avoid taking a loss and in hopes that the market will recover along with property values.

The last common ownership option is the Delaware Statutory Trust or DST. Because of its importance as a like-kind investment for §1031 exchanges, the next chapter is dedicated solely to this investment opportunity.

Chapter 13:
Unlock Hidden Assets Through a DST

"You can print money, manufacture diamonds, and people are a dime a dozen, but they'll always need land. It's the one thing they're not making any more of."

Evil villain Lex Luther in Superman I

Millions of Americans who own rental properties face a common challenge...*how to step down from the responsibilities of the landlord, without giving up the many benefits of income property ownership.*

Revenue Ruling 2004-86 was issued by the Treasury Department to permit a whole new way for investors to invest in fractional or co-ownership interests in real property. Under Revenue Ruling 2004-86, **Delaware Statutory Trusts or DSTs** are permitted to qualify as real estate and therefore as a replacement property solution for §1031 Exchange transactions. These statutory trusts are referred to as "Delaware" trusts because they are most often formed under the State of Delaware law.

The DST §1031 Exchange Solution

Many investors are familiar with §1031 exchanges that involve real property for real property and are performed by using a qualified intermediary. These exchanges are a great choice for investors who want to continue to be actively involved in their real estate portfolio. A Delaware Statutory Trust is a passive solution to satisfying a §1031 exchange.

Under IRS Revenue Ruling 2004-86, a DST can be used to acquire real estate, where the beneficial interests in the trust are treated as direct interests in replacement property for purposes of IRC §1031.

A DST is formed by a sponsoring firm, which organizes the trust, acquires the property under the trust umbrella, and becomes the master tenant and the manager/operator.

The investor **never** becomes a titled owner of the trust properties and never has any management obligations or control. Essentially, Rev. Proc. 2004-86 creates an exception to the general rule that a §1031 exchange seller cannot exchange from ownership of an entity which owns real estate into another such entity, or from direct-titled ownership into an entity which owns real estate.

A DST combines the ability of a §1031 exchange to defer taxes with ownership by multiple parties, typically facilitating larger investments such as multiple-unit apartment complexes, retail centers, large office buildings, etc., where economies of scale support professional management teams.

By sheltering gains from the sale of existing income producing real estate with a §1031 exchange, all of the equity built up over prior years can be invested in the DST. The investor does not lose purchasing power to federal and state taxes.

Simply put, DSTs provide hands-off, turn-key options for investors who may not have the time, energy, or real estate expertise to find investors and or manage a replacement property. And, DSTs can be used for a portion of the investor's real estate sales proceeds or 100% of the proceeds.

Top DST Benefits

- **No management responsibilities.** The DST is the single owner and decision maker on behalf of the investors.

- **Access to larger, institutional-quality properties.** DSTs allow investors to acquire partial ownership in multimillion-dollar properties that otherwise might be out of reach financially.

- **Limited personal liability.** The DST is the sole borrower.

- **Lower minimum investment requirements.**

- **Ability to diversify** §1031 exchange proceeds among multiple DSTs to achieve property type and geographic diversification.

- **Guarantee compliance** with §1031 exchange requirements when identifying a replacement property within the 45-day window becomes a problem.

- **Eliminate boot or excess cash** that might be left over from a §1031 exchange through the ability to invest remaining funds in a DST to avoid incurring taxes.

- **Allow for further §1031 exchanges.** The DST structure as a like-kind real estate investment allows funds to be exchanged over and over.

Structure of a DST

DST §1031 exchange offerings are generally sold as securities and are subject to federal securities regulations. Sponsors or syndicators offering DST §1031 exchange real estate investment opportunities must comply either by registering for a public offering or, more commonly, by making a "private offering" under SEC regulations.

1. The DST is formed through an initial offering in which investors can purchase interests in the trust.

   a. Up to 499 investors are allowed.

b. Offering documents specify the trust's investment strategy and disposition plans, i.e., when the property will be sold and the trust liquidated, typically between five and ten years.

2. DSTs are generally sold as securities, which requires that an investor work with a securities representative.

3. Once the offering is closed, there can be no future contributions to the DST by either current or new investors. The Trust executes its investment strategy.

When the IRS approved the DST structure for exchanges, it stipulated that the §1031 investors could not have any operational control or decision-making authority over the underlying properties. To protect investors, the IRS placed specific limits on the Trust that allow DSTs to qualify as suitable investments for the purpose of a tax-deferred §1031 exchange. These limits ensure the trustee distributes funds properly and does not take unnecessary risks with the DST's assets.

Seven Key Limits on a DST

1. Once the offering is closed, there can be no future equity contribution to the DST by either current or new co-investors or beneficiaries.

   • This prevents the original investors' ownership percentages from being diluted, reducing their claim to the DST's assets.

2. The trustee of the DST cannot renegotiate the terms of the existing loans, nor can it borrow any new funds from any other lender or party.

   • Protects the investor from additional liabilities that may not be within reason.

3. All proceeds earned by the DST must be distributed to the investors/beneficiaries rather than be reinvested.

- Ensures that beneficiaries have the right to determine how and when to reinvest or use the capital earned from their investment in the DST.

4. The trustee is limited to making capital expenditures with respect to the property to those for:

   - normal repair and maintenance
   - minor non-structural capital improvements
   - those required by law

5. Any liquid cash held in the DST between distribution dates can only be invested in short-term debt obligations, i.e. cash equivalents.

6. All cash, other than necessary reserves, must be distributed to the co-investors or beneficiaries on a current basis.

   - Protects the beneficiaries' rights to receive their income in a timely manner and use it as they choose.

7. The Trustee cannot enter into new leases or renegotiate the current leases.

   - Assures trustees will not make risky leasing decisions.
   - Allows for exceptions to be made in the case of a tenant bankruptcy or insolvency.

While these limitations help protect the beneficiaries' interests in the trust, they can also handicap the trust if the DST finds itself in danger of losing a property because the trustee is prohibited from taking necessary actions to remedy a problem.

To counteract this threat to the investor, the State of Delaware permits the DST to convert to a Limited Liability Company ("LLC"), if such provision is included in the origination documents. A "Springing LLC" has fewer operating restrictions, allowing the LLC manager to raise funds or renegotiate leases as necessary. The LLC structure also contains bankruptcy remote protections for the lender and the beneficiaries.

Because LLCs do not qualify as investments eligible to defer capital gains taxes through §1031 exchange, an LLC conversion can have considerable tax implications for investors. On the other hand, conversion may rescue a DST in danger and prevent heavy losses by the beneficiaries.

Useful Applications for a DST

Among the reasons to consider a §1031 exchange into a DST are:

Build net worth
— through appreciation in the value of the property

Experience cash flow from rental income
— after the cost of ownership, from maintenance and utilities to insurance, taxes, and property management

Pre-packaged approach
— access to quality real estate, with the property management team in place

Benefit from leverage
— real estate financing increases impact in appreciation on equity

Portfolio diversification
— real property backs the investment

Reduce net worth volatility
— real estate tends to have low correlation to stock movements

Reduce taxes
— depreciation allowance reduces current taxes

Simplify your life
— eliminate landlord duties for you and your family

Postpone capital gains and depreciation recovery taxes
— manage when you recognize taxes

Estate planning
— potentially eliminate capital gains and depreciation recovery taxes through a stepped-up basis for your heirs at your death

DST Due Diligence

While a DST may simplify the §1031 exchange and process of owning real estate, you still own real estate with all the risks of real estate.

Tenant vacancies, general market conditions and competition, interest rate risks, the risk of new supply coming to market and softening rental rates, general risks of owning/operating commercial and multifamily properties, short-term leases associated with multi-family properties, financing risks, potential adverse tax consequences, general economic risks, development risks and long hold periods can all impact the profitability of an investment, and the list goes on. As with any investment, there is the potential for loss as well as gain.

Due diligence means reading the offering documents and researching the offering company. A lack of operating history is a liability. Look for sponsor firms that have been in business and successfully completed deals. Have they sustained market downturns? Do they have a proven track record of acquiring, managing and disposing of assets for investors? Do they have a sizeable portfolio of real estate?

You also need to anticipate your potential need for liquidity. The average hold time of a §1031 DST investment is 5-7 years. This allows the §1031 DST sponsor time to gain appreciation in the property, and in turn provide appreciation returns to the investor.

What if you encounter the need the cash? While Delaware Statutory Trust liquidity is available, it is not a quick and easy process to liquidate of sell a fractional interest in a DST. Contact your advisor who facilitated the Delaware Statutory Trust paperwork. It may be possible to work with the DST §1031 Sponsor to find a buyer, but there are no guarantees.

1. If there is an interested buyer of your fractional interest, then the §1031 DST sponsor will coordinate the liquidity process of paperwork with the buyer.

2. If the DST §1031 sponsor cannot find a buyer in the Delaware Statutory Trust Liquidity process within the current portfolio, they may be willing to reach out to §1031 DST investors in other portfolios they administer.

3. If there are no interested buyers with the §1031 DST sponsor, then you will have to look outside the §1031 DST for a buyer.

Disadvantages of Owning a DST

Although a DST is an alternative to a standard replacement property acquisition, it may not fit every taxpayer's needs.

Liquidity is a key issue for investors. For other investors, the lack of control over the DST real estate may become an issue. The inability to refinance the property can force the manager to convert to an LLC structure to avoid major losses, triggering tax consequences for investors.

Before moving forward with this type of §1031 exchange using a DST, consult with your legal counsel, tax professional and financial advisor.

Chapter 14:

Investing Directly in Commercial Real Estate

"Buy on the fringe and wait. Buy land near a growing city! Buy real estate when other people want to sell. Hold what you buy."

John Jacob Astor

Many real estate investors are accidental investors. At one point they may have purchased a home that they later decided to turn into a rental property to generate monthly income or wanted to realize additional appreciation on the property in a high demand environment. The decision could also have resulted from a fall in real estate values when the owners were unable to recover the equity they had invested and opted to wait to sell in a more favorable market.

It's possible to be an accidental commercial real estate investor as well, typically by starting out with the purchase of a building for your own business. You may later want to trade up into a larger building using a §1031 to defer taxes or opt to convert your business property into a rental property.

There is a wide range of direct ownership commercial real estate investment opportunities available to consider from multi-family residential to office buildings and shopping centers. The catch is to make certain the transaction is in your best interest and fits your financial goals.

At Synergy, we take a holistic approach to buying real estate, both commercial and residential. This is an approach that looks at the property's impact on your financial future as well as your desire to own real estate that fits your lifestyle. This approach reflects our role as registered investment advisors through Synergy Asset Management, LLC and licensed real estate brokers through Synergy. Members of our company hold the Certified Financial Planner (CFP®) designation as well as certifications from other professional fields of study. We are in the unique position to offer both real estate and investment advice to help clients make sound real estate investment buying and selling decisions in the best interests of their long-term financial future.

Benefits of Commercial Real Estate

Real estate has long been a core portfolio holding for wealthy investors and a path to wealth for many individual investors. In addition to the ability to leverage the purchase of real estate and increase the impact of appreciation on your investment, real estate can offer on-going income and favorable risk-return tradeoffs that result from its uniqueness and the relatively inefficient markets in which real estate trades.

While higher risk, direct ownership of real estate tends to offer favorable risk-return tradeoffs that result from its uniqueness and the relatively inefficient markets in which real estate trades.

A commercial real estate investment allows you to:

1. Increase your net worth through appreciation in the value of the property.

2. Generate rental income, offsetting the costs of ownership, from maintenance and utilities to insurance, taxes, property management, and provide a steady cash flow.

3. Use the leverage provided by real estate financing to increase the benefit of appreciation.

4. Reduce current taxes by depreciating the value of the property over time.

5. Shelter from taxes gains from the profitable sale of a real estate investment through a 1031 exchange.

Before we discuss how to buy, sell, and hold commercial real estate, let's look at investor objectives, constraints and analysis of important features of real estate.

It is important to realize that commercial real estate is an entirely different game than investing in residential rental properties. Financing, lease terms, regulatory issues, building requirements, competition for tenants, market demand and supply are very different. Industry economics, business cycles and technological changes will matter more and you may find yourself involved in union and government negotiations.

Just as a mutual fund manager is responsible for managing securities for its shareholders, when you purchase real estate directly for investment, you are the manager. Your managerial decisions will greatly affect the returns earned from investing in real estate. Before you invest, ask yourself some tough questions.

Is your goal to invest in residential rentals and multifamily properties like apartments or commercial properties such as office buildings, retail complexes, storage units, parking lots, warehouses, industrial buildings, etc.?

You may be a real risk taker and prefer speculative property like raw land and real estate investment properties that are expected to provide returns primarily from appreciation in value due to location, scarcity, and so forth, rather than from periodic rental income.

If you decided on income producing property, you need to ask questions like:

- *What are the economics and physical requirements of the commercial market segment in which I am investing?*
- *Who will I be competing against for tenants?*
- *What rents should be charged?*
- *How much should be budgeted for maintenance and repairs?*
- *How will taxes affect my investment?*
- *Could future use of my real estate be restricted?*

- *What appurtenances will be transferred with the property?*
- *Are there any looming adverse environmental issues?*

Along with market forces, answers to such questions determine whether you will earn the desired return on a real estate investment. Remember, like other investment markets, the real estate market changes over time and you need to stay abreast of the macro and micro issues that might affect your real estate portfolio. Investing in real estate means more than just "buying right" or "selling right." It also means choosing the right properties for your investment needs and managing them well.

Managing your properties well will be easier if you have clearly identified your investment objectives and constraints. As we discussed earlier, do you want income producing property or speculative property? To select wisely, you need to consider the available types of properties, and to which type you are better suited.

When setting your objectives, you also need to set both financial and non-financial constraints and goals. Often this financial goal is stated in terms of discounted cash flows (net present value) or an internal rate of return (IRR). The risk-return relationship you find acceptable will be determined by:

- *How much money do you want to allocate to the real estate portion of your portfolio?*
- *Will you use debt financing?*
- *Do you require positive cash flow?*
- *How much down payment will you make or how much down payment is required to achieve your return goals?*
- *You also need to consider how your technical skills, temperament, repair skills, and managerial talents fit a potential investment.*
- *Do you want a building with curb appeal and that is trouble free?*
- *Or would you prefer a fixer-upper?*

The Real Estate Investment Policy Statement (RIPS)

Similar to a residential real estate investment, a holistic approach to commercial real estate investing starts with the Real Estate Investment Policy. The goal of the policy is to make certain the investment suits the investor's financial situation, investment goals and risk tolerance.

Investor motives:
1. Cash Flows
2. Tax planning
3. Appreciation
4. Hedge Inflation
5. Diversification
6. Emotional
7. Effects of leverage
8. Geographic location

The next step is understanding the investor in order to establish reasonable expectations, objectives, constraints, and guidelines in the investment of the portfolio's assets.

1. Why are they interested in owning investment property?

2. How long do they anticipate holding the property?

3. What are their expectations of the property in terms of personal involvement, cash flow and value?

4. Is their job likely to require relocation in the near future? If so, what might the timing look like?

5. When do they anticipate retiring? How will that impact their income requirements?

6. What are their financial goals?

Also considered are the buyer's business experience, technical skills, temperament, and repair skills. Is the individual suited to managing a property or is a hands-off approach more appropriate?

The policy also sets forth for the investors' understanding:

- Risk aspects of real estate investing

- Defines and describes the basic determinants of value in real estate

- Encourages effective communication between the investor and his commercial real estate asset management team

Analysis of Alternative Properties

At Synergy, we also focus on analyzing properties on the investor's behalf to determine which best suits the goals of the investor. Because Synergy has the capacity to model investment decisions, we help investors look at which property best fits their goals and at what price a purchase makes sense. Elements of the model are shown in Chapter 5.

This approach, based on the investor's desired rate of return, helps target appropriate properties and negotiate purchases that fit the financial capacity of the investor.

But first, let's look at a sample RIPS and some of the factors that will shape your investment decision.

SAMPLE RIPS

INVESTOR PROFILE:

Name	DOB	Occupation	Income	Net Worth
Jonathan Ward	12-7-66	Business Owner	$500,000	$3,000,000
Susan Ward	5-15-75	Spouse	$0	$3,000,000

Accredited Investor	YES	**Qualified Investor**	YES

INVESTOR SUMMARY:

Jonathan and Susan are interested in acquiring a real estate investment property to provide diversification to their liquid stock and bond portfolio. Their objective is to find a property that has the potential for capital appreciation and can produce both positive cash flow in the future.

INVESTOR MOTIVES:

Appreciation	Desire an increase in value over holding period.
Hedge Inflation	Desire a hedge against inflation.
Diversification	Seek diversification from low or uncorrelated returns to stock portfolio.
Emotional	Like the appeal of brick, mortar, curb appeal. Psychological security.
Effects of leverage	Desire to balance maximizing yield through leverage, with business risk.
Cash Flows	Positive net after tax cash flows if used as a rental.
Tax planning	Desire to minimize taxes on capital appreciation.
Geographic location	The West coast – Washington – greater Seattle area Safe area where Susan would feel comfortable visiting by herself late at night.

PORTFOLIO OBJECTIVES:

When setting your objectives, you also need to set both financial and non-financial constraints and goals. Often this financial goal is stated in terms of discounted cash flows (net present value) or an internal rate of return (IRR). You also need to consider how your technical skills, temperament, repair skills, and managerial talents fit a potential investment.

Time Horizon	Your time horizon is your projected or desired time to hold your investment property. Based on financial analysis, we can determine the optimal projected time to hold the investment. As specific property characteristics and market conditions change, the time horizon (holding period) should be reanalyzed. In general, directly owned real estate investments should have a longer holding period compared to other investments. Capital values fluctuate over shorter periods, and you should recognize that the possibility of capital loss does exist. However, historical asset class return data suggests that the risk of principal loss over a holding period of at least 10 to 20 years can be minimized. **TARGET TIME HORIZON: 7 YEARS**
Taxes	Taxes can affect the investment policy in several ways and should be analyzed by comparing pre-tax vs. post-tax opportunities, such as: • The determination as to the appropriate investment vehicles for a portfolio, either taxable or tax-free, and/or income producing or growth through capital appreciation. • The selection of either an active or passive strategy to be employed for a particular asset class and the manner in which the property is titled. Ordinary income and both short- and long-term capital gains taxes may apply.

Taxes (cont.)	As a result of deferred taxation, the after-tax return on commercial real estate typically is greater than an alternative investment with a comparable before tax yield. The cost-recovery deduction normally defers (and saves) taxes, an effect that is magnified by debt financing.
	Other issues to consider with your tax counsel are the effects of suspended losses and §1031 exchange opportunities.
	CURRENT TAX RATES:
	SHORT TERM CAPITAL GAINS: 39%
	LONG TERM CAPITAL GAINS: 0 – 25%
	RECAPTURE: 25%
Liquidity	Directly owned real estate is an illiquid investment and may take several years to sell. Moreover, reinvestment into the property may require further liquidity than projected. Considerations for working capital, capital improvements, and operating shortfalls should be carefully analyzed.
	Additionally, note a difference between marketability and liquidity. Marketability indicates the fact of "Salability", while liquidity indicates how fast that sale could occur at the current price. Marketability deals with getting the property ready for sale and making the sale, while liquidity focuses on realizing cash proceeds. Being illiquid does not necessarily mean non-marketable. It may still be sellable but not quickly or without loss, or a reduction in price.
Legal & Regulatory	We recommend that you seek the advice of an attorney for any concerns you may have regarding your real estate investment property's legal and regulatory constraints.

Unique Circumstances	Marketability of Assets: Due to the Investor's relatively long-term investment horizon, the Investor has determined that this Real Estate Investment Policy Statement can be invested in illiquid, long-term investments.
	Diversification: Investment of your funds shall be limited to the following categories:
	Permitted Asset Classes
	1. Apartments- Class A&B
	2. Industrial Properties
	3. Mixed Use
	4. Office
	Prohibited Asset Classes and/or Security Types
	1. Hotels
	2. Raw Land
	3. Development projects
	4. Retail
	When and if applicable, this RIPS should reference the NCREIF property index to gain insight to property performance indicators.
Return Objective	**Total return: Current yield plus appreciation.**
	Further, returns can be considered in nominal terms and in real terms. Nominal returns include inflation and real returns adjust the return without inflation.
	Returns can also be examined on both a pre-tax and post-tax basis, and before and after debt.
	Via financial modeling, scenario and sensitivity analysis, and Monte Carlo simulation, we can fully explore a range of possible portfolio outcomes.
	IRR YIELD REQUIREMENT: 12% -15%
	NPV PROFILE: POSITIVE

Risk	Investment theory and historical capital market return data suggest that, over long periods of time, there is a relationship between the level of risk assumed and the level of return that can be expected in an investment portfolio. In general, higher risk (e.g., volatility of return) is associated with higher return. Returns can also be evaluated by comparing relative returns to absolute returns.
	Given this relationship between risk and return, a fundamental step in determining the investment policy for the Portfolio is the determination of an appropriate risk tolerance. There are two primary factors that affect the Investor's risk tolerance:
	Financial ability to accept risk within the investment portfolio and willingness to accept return volatility
	Taking these two factors into account and based on previous inputs concerning investment time horizon and cash flow needs, the Investor rates his or her own risk tolerance as:
	Possessing the ability to seek both modest capital appreciation and income from their portfolio. This investor will have either a moderate time horizon or a slightly higher risk tolerance. While this range is still designed to preserve the investor's capital, fluctuations in the values of portfolio may occur from year to year.
	Please recognize that higher returns involve some volatility and you must have a willingness to tolerate declines in the value of your real estate portfolio.
	Risk is discussed further in the section Evaluating Risk.

The RIPS is intended to be a summary of an investment philosophy and the procedures that provide guidance for the investors and their financial professionals. These policies should reflect the investors' current status and philosophy regarding the investment of the real estate portion of their portfolio.

The RIPS also cautions the investor that there can be no guarantee about the attainment of the goals or investment objectives outlined herein.

The Importance of Working with a Registered Investment Advisor

Real estate brokers and consultants are not authorized to give investment advice unless they are also a registered investment advisor. A real estate license allows the broker to bring a willing buyer and willing seller together, and to assist them in completing a transaction. They cannot legally offer investment advice.

Investing in commercial real estate is a big step for individuals and takes the pressure up a notch from starting with a residential property with the goal of transitioning it into a rental property. More than ever, qualified advice is essential. When you work with a fee-based registered investment advisor you work with a financial professional who takes a fiduciary position in the relationship. Your interest as the client comes first. That is a level of advice beyond "Is it suitable?" The question becomes "Is it in the best interest of the individual?"

As you walk through the steps of determining what level of commercial investing you want to take on and how to select the right property, make certain you have the right advice and the knowledge to analyze and evaluate the properties that interest you and to help you find the right financing and ownership structure.

Directly Owned Real Estate's Position in the Investment Portfolio

- Diversification
- Tangible asset — value is driven primarily by economic fundamentals
- Total Return — Potential for dependable, steady cash flow and liquidity through rent income, plus appreciation
- Inflation protector given ability to adjust rental rates upward when inflation rises

Finding the Right Property — Primary Features to Consider

There are four general features related to real estate investments on which to base your analysis.

PHYSICAL PROPERTY
PROPERTY RIGHTS
HOLDING PERIOD
LOCATION

Physical Property

Through proper inspection of the site and its building(s), you can make sure you are buying what you think you are buying. Problems can arise if you fail to obtain a site survey, an accurate square footage measurement, or an inspection of the building(s). Be sure to confirm that the purchase and sale agreement accurately identifies the real estate via its legal description and that it lists all items of personal property you expect to receive (such as a refrigerator).

Property Rights

When you buy real estate, what you are really buying is a bundle of legal rights that fall under concepts in law such as deeds, titles, easements, liens, and encumbrances. Just like you do a physical inspection, you want to do a legal inspection. Real estate and lease agreements should not be the work of amateurs, and you should seek the advice of a qualified attorney when necessary.

Holding Period

When you are evaluating your holding period or time horizon, you need to remember that the real estate market goes through cycles just like other markets do, and you need to identify where you are in the cycle. Prices go up and down, slowly and quickly, so before judging whether prices will appreciate or depreciate, decide what time period is relevant for your situation and the property in which you are investing.

Location

Location, location, location! You have heard it before, and, yes, it really is that important. For some properties, the area of greatest concern consists of a few blocks. For others, an area of hundreds of square miles serves as the relevant market area. Understand the boundaries that are important for your investment so you can properly analyze supply and demand.

Determinants of Value

The last issue I will mention before moving on is determinants of value. In the analysis of real estate investments, as with all investments, valuation is a key concern. This subject matter could go on for pages; but I will keep my comments brief, because I feel you should be working with a qualified professional who can help you with valuation issues.

There are three main determinants of value that will help you evaluate your real estate investment.

DEMAND
SUPPLY
THE PROPERTY

Demand

Demand is the measurement of people's desire to buy or rent a given property at a given time and stems from a market area's economic base. Property values follow an upward path when employment is increasing, and values typically fall when employers begin to lay off workers. Population demographics and people's emotional dispositions called psychographics are also key elements to demand.

Supply

How many other similar properties (competitors) are available in your targeted area? Size up the competition. The more properties on the market for a given number of buyers or sellers, the lower the value becomes. The fewer properties on the market, the higher the value becomes. One other concept to evaluate is the principle of substitution. Are there other properties that can fill the same need? If so, then there is more supply.

The Property

The property itself is a key ingredient. Look for a property's unique selling advantage. What makes it different? What is its competitive edge? Investors should consider five factors:

- Restrictions on the use of the property
- The location
- The size and quality of the site
- Improvements made
- The efficiency of management

Once you have gathered all the pertinent valuation determinants, you can then perform the valuation and investment analysis, interpret your results, and make a portfolio decision.

To Summarize the Process

1. Set objectives, goals, and constraints
2. Analyze important features of the property
3. Gather determinants of value
4. Perform analysis
5. Implement your decision

Financing Commercial Real Estate

Commercial real estate loans tend to fall into five categories: SBA 7(a) loans, CDC/SBA 504 loans, traditional commercial real estate mortgages, commercial bridge loans, and commercial hard money loans. Each type of loan has specific terms and qualifications making them suitable for a variety of commercial property needs. Rates and terms shown in the following charts reflects those available early in 2020.

SBA 7(a) Loan	Long-term commercial real estate loan up to $5 million
CDC / SBA 504 Loan	Commercial real estate loans no maximum loan amount
Traditional Mortgage	Commercial real estate loans no maximum loan amount
Commercial Bridge Loan	Short-term commercial real estate financing
Commercial Hard Money Loan	Bad credit option for short-term renovation financing

SBA 7(a) Loan for Commercial Real Estate

Maximum Loan Amount	$5 million
Minimum Down Payment	10% to 20%
Interest Rates	7.5% to 10%
SBA Guarantee Fee	2% to 3.75% (of guaranteed portion)
Closing Costs	2% to 5%
Maximum Loan Term	25 years
Time to Approval / Funding	60 to 90 days
Minimum Credit Score	680
Years in Business	2 years
Debt-Service Coverage Ratio	1.25x or greater
Owner-Occupancy Requirement	at least 51%

These are long-term loans, making them a good fit for buy-and-hold investors. They are designed to help businesses that are unable to obtain credit elsewhere. Before applying, review the SBA loan qualification requirements to ensure that your business is eligible.

SBA loan rates are capped by the Small Business Administration and are tied to the prime rate. The loans can have fixed or variable interest rates, making it important for borrowers to verify with their lender the type of rate they are receiving. SBA guarantee fee, closing costs, and appraisal fees are typically taken directly out of the loan. There may be a prepayment penalty if you pay off more than 25% of the loan within the first three years.

The Small Business Administration sets basic qualification requirements for SBA loans and allows lenders to set their own eligibility requirements beyond those specifications. Determining factors such as credit score, time in business, and annual revenue requirements are set by the lender, and therefore may vary.

CDC/SBA 504 Loan For Commercial Real Estate

Backed by the U.S. Small Business Administration. CDC/SBA 504 loans help new and existing businesses purchase or refinance an owner-occupied commercial property. A CDC/SBA 504 loan is comprised of two loans, one from a Certified Development Corporation (CDC) and one from a traditional lender. The maximum loan amount for CDC/SBA 504 loans is $14 million.

Maximum Loan Amount	$14 million
Minimum Down Payment	10% to 20%
Interest Rates	4.5% to 6% on CDC loan 5% to 12% on bank loan
SBA Guarantee Fee	approximately 1%
CDC Processing Fee	1% to 2% (CDC portion)
Closing Costs	2% to 5%
Typical Loan Term	20 years

Time to Approval / Funding	60 to 90 days
Minimum Credit Score	680
Years in Business	at least 2 years
Debt-Service Coverage Ratio	1.25x or greater
Owner-Occupancy Requirement	at least 51%

CDC / SBA 504 loans for commercial real estate typically provide financing for up to 90% of the purchase price of the property, with a maximum term of 20 years, and consists of fully amortizing principal and interest payments.

Traditional Commercial Mortgage

A traditional commercial mortgage is a standard commercial loan issued by a bank or lending institution and not backed by the federal government. Traditional commercial mortgages can be used to purchase or refinance real estate such as owner-occupied office buildings, retail centers, shopping centers, industrial warehouses, and other commercial properties.

Maximum Loan Amount	65% to 85% Loan-to-Value (LTV)
Minimum Down Payment	15% to 35%
Interest Rates	5% to 7%
Origination Fees	0% to 1%
Closing Costs	2% to 5%
Typical Loan Term	5 to 20 years
Time to Approval / Funding	30 to 45 days
Minimum Credit Score	700
Years in Business	1 to 5 years

Debt-Service Coverage Ratio	1.25x or greater
Owner-Occupancy Requirement	At least 51%

Qualifications for a traditional commercial mortgage are a little more restrictive than with a government-backed loan because the lender assumes the full risk of the loan. There is no insurance provided by a government guarantee.

When applying for a traditional commercial mortgage, you should expect to have the following:

Commercial Bridge Loan

A commercial bridge loan is a short-term real estate loan used to purchase owner-occupied commercial property before refinancing to a long-term mortgage at a later date.

Loan Amount	$2 million to $20 million
Minimum Down Payment	10% to 20% of Loan-to-Value (LTV)
Starting Interest Rates	8% to 12%
Loan Origination Fees	2% to 6%
Closing Costs	2% to 5%
Exit Fee	1%
Typical Loan Term	6 months to 36 months
Time to Approval / Funding	15 to 45 days
Minimum Credit Score	650
Debt Service Coverage Ratio	1.10x or greater
Prior Commercial Projects	1 to 3

Monthly payments on a commercial bridge loan are typically interest-only, with the full amount of principal repaid at the end of the term. Repayment terms range from six months to 36 months.

Commercial Hard Money Loan

A commercial hard money loan is a short-term loan used to purchase — and sometimes renovate — a commercial property before refinancing with long-term commercial real estate loan. Hard money loans often used by real estate investors looking to renovate a building before refinancing to a permanent mortgage or to help borrowers compete with all-cash buyers.

Maximum Loan Amount	Up to 80% LTV Up to $2.5 million
Minimum Down Payment	15% to 35%
Interest Rates	8% to 12%
Origination Fees	2% to 5%
Closing Costs	2% to 5%
Prepayment Penalty	1%
Typical Loan Term	1 to 3 years
Time to Approval / Funding	10 to 15 days
Minimum Credit Score	600
Prior Commercial Projects	1 to 3

Different Types of Commercial Real Estate Leases

Residential leases are relatively simple. The tenant pays a fixed monthly rent plus utilities as determined by the lease. Commercial real estate leases tend to fall into four main categories but may also be a blend of lease styles.

- Gross Lease
- Triple Net Lease
- Modified Net Lease
- Percentage Lease

The Gross Lease

A gross lease is commonly used with office buildings with multiple tenants. There is a fixed monthly rent and tenants may pay some utilities, such as telephone and data. The landlord picks up the cost of building maintenance and most operating expenses. The lease might include a load factor or percentage of costs associated with maintaining common areas, such as a lobby or conference rooms based on the share of the overall building that the tenant occupies.

The Double, Triple and Absolute Net Lease

A Double Net lease may require the tenant to pay base rent plus taxes and insurance. A Triple Net (NNN) lease adds a third cost — a significant share of the expenses of the operation. The triple net lease might be used when the tenant is a heavy utility user, engages in activities that could increase insurance costs or imposes a level of operating cost uncertainty on the property owner. An "Absolute Lease" passes financial responsibility for the entire building onto the tenant.

The Modified Net Lease

The modified net lease is a compromise between a gross lease and a triple net lease. It enables landlords and tenants to customize lease terms that meet the needs of both parties.

The Percentage Lease

A percentage lease includes a base rent plus an additional percentage of monthly sales volumes. This can work well for a retail store where summer months are considerably less profitable than the Christmas holiday season.

Unlike the residential market, where individual states may have a standardized lease, commercial leases can be whatever the landlord and tenant agree to, with satisfactory terms can reflecting one or more variations.

Integrating Financial Analysis in the Real Estate Decision

Commercial real estate investing demands the in-depth financial analysis Synergy provides with its structured approach to modeling investment returns over a 15-year holding period. Our professional focus is on analyzing investment real estate alternatives for clients to help them build efficient portfolios designed to allow them to meet their financial goals.

We want our clients select and hold high quality investments that meet their return objectives and manage the risk of the investment underperforming.

Real Estate Transfer Process

This is the process of promotion and negotiation of the property, which can significantly influence the cash flows a property will provide. Here we are trying to bring efficiency to an inefficient market. You may want to think of this as creative or efficient marketing. By understanding the financial characteristics of commercial properties through our valuation model, we are able to establish at what price a property makes sense and work with sellers to negotiate competitive pricing.

Cautions to Take to Heart

It's important to realize that when you enter the commercial real estate market you are competing with companies that have spent years and considerable investment in their specialized markets. Take your time to learn as much as possible about the niche you wish to fill before investing. Understand your risks. Know your potential tenants and their business models. If there is an opportunity to work with a company in the commercial real estate field that serves the niche you want to enter, it may be well worth it to spend some time as an employee before you invest.

There are considerable rewards from a successful real estate investment, but those rewards are not guaranteed. Commercial real estate comes with risks to balance those rewards. The more knowledge you have of your investment market, the better the odds that you will be successful. Build a team of good advisors who will help you make good decisions.

Chapter 15:

Using Your IRA to Finance Investment Real Estate

"Buy land, they aren't making anymore of it."

Mark Twain

Most people don't realize they have a choice outside of the typical type of Wall Street investment such as stocks, bonds, mutual funds, ETFs, fixed income instruments, etc. when investing their retirement funds. Even most investment professionals don't know an Individual Retirement Account (IRA) can be used to purchase alternative investments such as real estate. If anything, they're more likely to advise against such an investment because they have been ill-informed and are not properly educated about this option.

Because they don't understand how to use an IRA in this manner, and because they've only heard about how difficult and dangerous it can be, and because they won't get a commission, they advise against investing your IRA in alternative assets.

A self-directed IRA permits the use of IRA funds for alternative investments including real estate. Self-directed means you have control over what you want to invest in, how you want to invest in it, and how much you choose to invest.

Funding Real Estate Investments With Retirement Savings

For many years now, people have been using non-directly owned real estate in their IRAs and other retirement plans. These intangibles are investments like REITs and real estate mutual funds. But it is also possible to use retirement plans to purchase directly owned real estate such as raw land, commercial buildings, condos, residential properties, empty lots, trust deeds, or real estate contracts.

In general, the internal revenue code (IRC) section 408 does not prohibit the holding of real estate in an IRA, provided the transaction is not prohibited under IRC Section 4975.

PROHIBITED IRA TRANSACTIONS

Code section 4975 covers what transactions are prohibited between an IRA or retirement plan and a "disqualified person." Generally, "disqualified persons" are defined to be the accountholder, other fiduciaries, certain family members, and businesses under the accountholder's control.

IRC Sec. 4975: An IRA cannot engage in any transaction (direct or indirect) with anybody or anything considered related to the IRA.

- A self-directed IRA/Solo 401k may not purchase a property that the account holder owns. By the same token, the account holder cannot buy a property owned by the IRA/Solo 401(k).

- The account holder cannot live in, or vacation in, a property that the IRA/Solo 401(k) owns.

- The account holder cannot hire a business owned by a disqualified person to provide a service to the IRA/Solo 401(k) owned property. In other words, if the IRA owns a rental property, the account holder cannot hire his father's roofing company to replace the roof.

- The account holder cannot receive a salary for managing the property. However, s/he may perform managerial services without charging the IRA or Solo 401(k) a fee. (These duties fall under responsibilities of the non-compensated manager of the LLC or Trustee.)

- The account holder cannot perform physical work to a property that the IRA or Solo 401(k) owns. The reason for this restriction is that the work would be considered a non-cash contribution to the IRA or Solo 401(k), which is prohibited, and is commonly referred to as Sweat Equity.

- Any loan obtained by the IRA to purchase real estate must be a nonrecourse loan. A nonrecourse loan is a loan where the lender's sole recourse in the event of default is to foreclose and take the property back.

In essence, the prohibited transaction rules prohibit an IRA or qualified retirement plan from owning a piece of property which will be purchased from or used personally by the accountholder, family members, or businesses under the accountholder's control. Simply put, the property must be used for investment purposes only and cannot be used personally while maintained in the IRA. In addition, properties that are individually owned outside of the IRA cannot be transferred or purchased by one's individual IRA.

As the IRA holder, you are not allowed to use your IRA funds to purchase property which you use for your primary residence, or a vacation home. You are a "disqualified person." You are not allowed to live in any real estate investment you own through your IRA. There are a number of other restrictions, too. Your spouse is also disqualified, and so are all your lineal ascendants and descendants and all their spouses and children. Your father, grandfather, great-grandfather and their spouses, and all your children, and your children's children and all their spouses are all disqualified. When it comes to personally benefiting yourself or your family through the ownership of real estate, you are all considered disqualified.

Nor will the IRS let your business lease property from your IRA. You cannot have personal use or benefit from the property. If you did, it could cost you plenty in taxes and penalties.

A disqualified person who takes part in a prohibited transaction must correct the transaction and must pay an excise tax based on the amount involved in the transaction. The initial tax on a prohibited transaction is 15% of the amount involved for each year (or part of a year) in the taxable period. If the transaction is not corrected within the taxable period, an additional tax of 100% of the amount involved is imposed. Both taxes are payable by any disqualified person who participated in the transaction (other than a fiduciary acting only as such). If more than one person takes part in the transaction, each person can be jointly and severally liable for the entire tax.

The amount involved in a prohibited transaction is the greater of the following amounts:

- The money and fair market value of any property given
- The money and fair market value of any property received

If services are performed, the amount involved is any excess compensation given or received.

It may make sense, however, to take the property out of the IRA as a distribution and live in it during retirement. Make sure not to move in until the distribution is complete. The distribution would need to be at the current market value as of the date of distribution and taxes would be due unless your account was a Roth IRA. This may be a good reason to convert your IRA to a Roth. Further, if you were under the age 59½, a 10% penalty may also apply.

EXAMPLE: Convert your IRA to a Roth IRA and pay the income taxes now. Once the conversion is complete, use your new Roth IRA to purchase a residential rental property in a location in which you may want to retire. Rent the property until retirement. When you are ready to retire, take the property out of the Roth IRA as a tax-free distribution, assuming you follow the rules, and then you may live in the property.

For those of you who stopped reading and immediately called your basic IRA provider so you could get started investing in real estate right away, you probably were told that you were not allowed to do so and now think I'm crazy. So, now that you're back, let's find out how you go about doing this.

Open a Self-Directed IRA

The first key step to investing tax-deferred or tax-exempt in real estate is to open a self-directed IRA with any one of the dozen or so independent IRA custodians that allow real estate investments.

A self-directed IRA is simply an IRA where you are in control of your investment options and are not limited to just stocks, bonds, mutual funds, and other traditional securities.

In a self-directed IRA, you have access to all of these traditional investments plus real estate and even other alternative asset classes.

Not all IRA custodians offer the alternative investment option. Only some do, and you'll have to do your due diligence to find them and find out if they accept IRA investments in real estate. When you find an alternative custodian, also find out how long they've been in business, and investigate their track record in this asset area. These custodians won't be that hard to find and some have been in existence since IRAs were first offered about five decades ago.

THREE LEVELS OF ALTERNATIVE ASSET CUSTODIANS

Something to be aware of when you are thinking about establishing a self-directed IRA is that the term "self-directed" is a marketing term, it's not an official or actual name of a retirement account and is no different from a traditional IRA account. The way it works is that a trust custodian is responsible for the qualified IRA plans. When you want to use your IRA funds to invest in real estate, you have to find a custodian that allows alternative investing in real estate or other types of alternative assets. That's the difference.

Some custodians will accept IRA alternative investments in real estate, and others may specialize only in private mortgages, private company stock, oil and gas resources, Limited Partnerships, precious metals, equine opportunities, or intellectual property. There is a host of alternative investments available to you through your self-directed IRA.

There are three different levels of entities that hold alternative assets.

1. **The foremost entity is the trust custodian.** The trust custodians are overseen by the Securities and Exchange Commission (SEC), and the assets they monitor are in the billions of dollars.

2. **Under the trust custodians are the administrators.** These are the entities that actually hold the assets, the administrative arm that acts as a record keeper for the trust custodian. The trust custodian monitors the work of the administrators to ensure that all records are kept accurately, and the funds are secure.

3. **Below the administrators are the facilitators.** Their responsibility is to provide consulting and advice.

You can still make contributions to your self-directed IRA account, and when you get older you can accelerate your contributions just as you can with traditional IRAs. Under the SECURE Act of 2019, when you reach 72 years of age, you're required to take the required minimum distribution — calculated according to your age and the amount of money in your account — unless you have a Roth IRA.

The custodian holds the papers on your real estate investment, and any investment income that's received from your property is deposited into your IRA. The custodian is responsible for all paperwork and records, pays out all the investment expenses, and will also help you roll your IRA value into a traditional IRA or any other form of government authorized retirement plan that's appropriate when you are ready to convert.

Because fees and other services may vary, it is a good idea to check out a few of the independent IRA custodians to find the one that fits best with your needs.

Now that you know how to open an account, let's discuss how to fund the account. In 2020, the IRA and Roth IRA contribution limit is $6,000 or $7,000 for an individual over the age of 50 and making catch up contributions. We all know that six or seven thousand dollars is not enough to buy a rental house, so how else can we fund the IRA?

You can fund the IRA through a direct rollover from an existing IRA or 401(k) plan, if eligible, into a new self-directed IRA, also called a trustee-to-trustee rollover. Funds are moved electronically from one account to another without any action on your part.

With an indirect rollover, you receive a check which you must deposit in an approved retirement plan within 60 calendar days of withdrawal. If the check isn't deposited by then, it's treated as an early distribution, subject to additional taxes and penalties. Financial institutions often withhold taxes (generally 20%) on indirect rollovers. When you deposit the check into a new retirement account, make sure you also deposit an amount equal to the taxes withheld in Box 4 of your 1099-R. If you don't, the Box 4 amount may be treated as an early distribution. (In the meantime, the Box 4 amount will either be added to your refund or applied to your tax liability, so everything will even out in the end.)

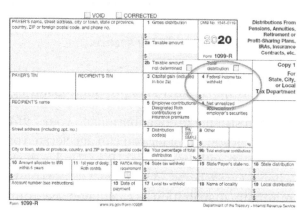

In many scenarios, the IRA holder will have sufficient funds to cover the real estate purchase, but what if you find a great investment property for your IRA, something really valuable, and your retirement account simply doesn't have adequate funds? Luckily, there are ways in which you can make the purchase and still keep the transaction both legal and profitable.

LEVERAGING REAL ESTATE INVESTING WITH YOUR IRA

There are banks that will give you a loan on an asset owned by an IRA. When you buy real estate with your IRA account, you may be able to get leverage on the asset and qualify for a non-recourse mortgage. A non-recourse mortgage means you are not personally guaranteeing the loan, and the property itself is the only collateral. The lender has no recourse for full repayment if the collateral is insufficient to pay the debt.

To do so legally, you must use the IRA-purchased property, not the IRA itself, as security for the loan. A non-recourse loan is not like the loan on your personal residence. In fact, it is very different. Here, unlike your home loan, if the loan isn't paid back as promised, the lender may foreclose on the IRA-owned property used to secure the debt but may not take recourse against any of your other assets. Because of its unique nature, not very many banks or lending institution offer these types of loans, but they do exist, and your self-directed IRA custodian may be able to point you in the right direction.

Like other loans, non-recourse loans do have a monthly payment and some type of amortization schedule which will need to be followed. Therefore, your IRA property will need to be able to make the loan payments from the property's cash flow, your annual IRA contributions (within the 2020 limits — $6,000 or $7,000 if 50 or over), or some combination of the two. Simply put, you need to have more money coming into your IRA than is going out. This also means you need to have sufficient liquidity in your IRA for other real estate-related expenses like property taxes, insurance, and other repairs and maintenance. Remember, the IRA itself must pay all expenses. Let's look at a simple example:

Present Value of Loan $100K

Term (amortization period)	30-year fixed
Annual Interest Rate	7%
Monthly Payment	$665.30
Annual Payment	$7,983.62
Annual Property Tax	$1,500
Annual Insurance Premium	$400
Annual Repairs	$150
TOTAL ANNUAL COSTS = $10,033.62	

The amount of $10,033.62 is the amount of money going out each year, and so your property would need to have more than this amount coming in each year. So, for a person under the age of 50, you could subtract the $6,000 annual IRA contribution from the $10,033.62 annual expenses and you would need ($10,033.62 - $6,000 = $4,033.62) $4,033.62 of cash flow from the property.

What if your property generates a positive cash flow?

There are some special tax considerations to be aware of. One is **UBIT — Unrelated Business Income Tax.** If unrelated business income is $1,000 or more per year, the IRS requires reporting of the UBTI on Form 990-T and the payment of excise tax.

According to IRS Publication 598, "If an exempt organization regularly carries on a trade or business not substantially related to its exempt purpose, except that it provides funds to carry out that purpose, the organization is subject to tax on its income from that unrelated trade or business."

There are exceptions, and most income generated by passive investments is exempt from paying UBTI, including income from dividends, annuities, royalties, interest from loans and most rent generated from real estate. One way an IRA investment could generate UBTI is the use of IRA funds to flip properties, since the property is considered inventory and not investments.

The second tax consideration is **UDFI — Unrelated Debt Financed Income** — which is a tax levied on the portion of profits that can be attributed to leverage. For example:

"Another way that UBTI is generated is through debt-financed income (also known as UDFI). UDFI occurs in a case like this: An IRA purchases a piece of real estate to be held for rental property. In the purchase of the property, the IRA put 50% down in cash and financed the remaining 50% through the seller. Even though rental income is considered exempt, since debt was used to acquire the property, half of the rental income (reducing as the debt is paid off) would be considered UDFI, and therefore subject to taxation." The good news is that the proportional part of the expenses associated with the debt-financed income would offset the income.

If you use leverage or generate income from an IRA investment which is not related to the main purpose of the investment, it is best to consult a tax professional. A tax professional will ensure the registration and Tax Identification Number on the Schedule K-1 are correct and prepare Form 990-T to submit to your IRA custodian. Once completed, you can then provide the Form 990-T to your IRA custodian with your authorization to file the form and pay the UBTI from your IRA account.

The Purchasing Process

Now we are ready to talk about how to actually purchase the property. When using your IRA to purchase property, the steps in buying real estate are really no different than if you were not using your IRA. There are a few things to be aware of, and we will review them now.

THE BASIC STEPS ARE

- The Purchase and Sales Agreement (the offer)
- The Acceptance
- The Inspection
- The Closing

The purchase and sales agreement is where it all starts and is probably the most important step. Each self-directed IRA custodian will have their own set of rules and procedures, so you need to review their real estate processing checklist well in advance of making an offer.

You need to make sure that the purchase is made by your IRA custodian and not you, personally. This means that you will need to set up your self-directed IRA prior to making an offer. If you are under the gun and did not have time to open your IRA, and if the person making the offer is not a disqualified person, you may make the offer in the following way: "John Doe and or assigns." Adding the phrase "and or assigns" will allow you to assign the contract to the IRA custodian once the account opened.

In addition, if you put up earnest money with your personal funds, you will need to make sure you include that amount in the total due so that the title company can reimburse you upon closing.

Some IRA custodians will require that they hold the original recorded title to the property in safekeeping. The title should reflect the name of your IRA custodian for your benefit, such as, XYZ Trust Company, Custodian FBO John Smith IRA.

Some investors make the mistake of fully utilizing their IRA funds to purchase a property, leaving nothing in reserve to cover maintenance costs. Most properties will have some costs of this sort, and although profit distributions will eventually help to cover them, it is not wise to assume that the timing will work out perfectly.

The funds to cover costs must come from the IRA, not from the account holder's pocket. That would be a Prohibited Transaction and could have negative repercussions for the IRA. The easiest way to avoid this problem is to calculate the property-related outlay for the upcoming year and make sure that there is an equivalent cash amount in the IRA account.

FOLLOW THE RULES

Having a self-directed IRA is like having a fancy red roadster. People will notice! When you take it out on the highway, are you going to speed? Do you think there may be someone waiting out there to enforce the law?

If you get audited, the IRS will ask if you have any IRAs. Then they'll ask how you invested your IRAs. They'll show interest when you tell them you have a self-directed IRA. You'll be asked about the investments you made in your self-directed IRA, and since they know the rules and regulations of what you're allowed to buy, they'll check to see if you employed a financial planner to guide you. Eventually their inquiries will lead them to conclude you either did or did not commit a direct or indirect violation. The point here is there are obstacles and pitfalls to avoid, and unless you're a tax attorney or a CPA specializing in IRAs and tax law, it's possible your best strategy could be to hire the services of an experienced fee-based financial planner.

Stick to the rules and regulations so you don't put your finances in harm's way. Even if you don't get caught and your IRA goes to your beneficiary, if they get audited, they may have to take a distribution and pay the tax, penalty and the interest.

You certainly don't want to harm the well-being of your loved ones, so it's always best to stay within the legally prescribed limitations. You worked hard to get this money into its qualified status, so there is no sense making trouble for yourself or the ones you care about when you can actually do so much good instead.

Remember that investing in real estate is like any other investment. You have to know what you're doing, you have to know the market, you have to work with experienced qualified professionals, and you have to accept that your investment, like every investment, has risk. You can suffer losses as well as rejoice over gains. Using your self-directed

IRA account for alternative investing is simply a device for accessing funds about which most investment professionals aren't sufficiently educated or experienced.

In conclusion, I hope you now realize that there are some interesting and creative ways to invest in real estate and that this can be done in your IRA or other types of retirement plans. This topic is very complex and by no means have all the elements of this opportunity been covered in the article, but I hope it was a good start for you.

Please remember that this type of investing is best utilized when using a team of professionals that can help you navigate the potential hazards. Seek the advice from the following professionals as needed: an Attorney, CPA, IRA Custodian, CFP, Real Estate professional, Mortgage Broker, Registered Investment Advisor or other competent Financial Advisor.

Chapter 16:

In Summary

"Most of the successful people I've known are the ones who do more listening than talking."

Bernard Baruch

Investing real estate is addicting. It's an opportunity to shape your environment, to create a stream of income that pays you even while you sleep, and to have something tangible at the end of the day that will be there no matter what else the financial markets are doing.

Risk is always a part of every real estate investment, whether it is the risk of a natural disaster, a man-made disaster, changing markets or a bad decision. But with real estate, you have a chance to control to some degree the final outcome. And that seems more and more a rarity in today's world.

In addition to conveying the tremendous opportunity we see in real estate investing, we also want to stress the importance of:

- Knowing why you are investing and what you want to achieve
- Understanding your financial limits
- Building a real estate team that will help you succeed

While real estate investing may sometimes be an accident of life, you want to go into every transaction with as much knowledge and understanding of the market and the property as you can. This is much easier to achieve when you have access to a team of high-quality professionals who can help with the various stages of purchasing, managing and selling your property.

A holistic approach to real estate investment means this team also includes your financial advisor. It's easy to become overextended. And it's difficult to know everything there is about your investment property and its potential. But you can find experienced professionals who will help you fill in the gaps in your personal knowledge and experience.

Estate Planning and Real Estate

In addition to real estate's advantages of —

- Leveraging appreciation through debt financing
- Generating income
- Tax Advantages

Real estate can be very useful in estate planning.

Under 2020 estate tax laws, real estate is stepped up to market value when inherited. That means the value of a property is determined based on current market conditions for the purposes of valuing an estate and subsequent estate taxes. It passes to your heirs at that value. This has the effect of eliminating up to four different taxes:

- Depreciation recapture at a rate of 25%
- Federal long-term capital gain taxed at either 20% or 15% depending on taxable income
- 3.8% net investment income tax ("NIIT") when applicable
- Applicable state tax rate (as high as an additional 13.3% in California)

Under the 2017 Tax Cuts & Jobs Act (TCJA), individuals can leave an estate of up to $11.2 million exempt of federal estate taxes (state-level estate taxes may still apply).

With the passage of the SECURE Act, December 20, 2019, inheriting a retirement account became much less attractive due to the law's requirement that inherited retirement accounts be liquidated within 10 years. The act eliminated the ability of heirs to "stretch" the inherited account out over their lifespan, thus creating a steady flow of income. This has made leaving retirement accounts to children and grandchildren much less advantageous.

One way to leave a steady flow of income to children and grandchildren can be income-producing real estate. This might include a single property or multiple properties. Utilizing a 1031 exchange, the property owner might diversify into multiple properties with each property assigned to a different heir.

In 2020, the estate and gift tax exemption is $11.58 million per individual. That means a real estate investor can leave $11.58 million in highly appreciated real estate to heirs and pay no federal estate or gift tax. A married couple can shield $23.16 million. This is an area to discuss with your estate planner, but it does offer one way to never pay federal taxes on gains from your real estate investments.

I hope the information in this book gives you a good starting point for building a real estate portfolio. To recap:

1. Set objectives, goals, and constraints

2. Build a team of experienced professionals to help you implement your plan

3. Analyze the market in which you plan to invest

4. Understand important features of the property

5. Gather determinants of value — Is there demand? What is the supply situation? Is this the right property for the market and your needs

6. Analyze the financial consequences of your purchase, both short and long-term

7. Implement your decision

Good luck in your future as a property owner and if we can be of assistance to you, don't hesitate to give Synergy a call.

Appendix — Resources

Maas, Joseph M. (2014) *Exit Insight: Getting to "Sold!"* Merrell Marketing.

Maas, Joseph M. (2015) *Exit Insight: Getting to "Retired!"* Merrell Marketing.

Index

Made in the USA
Middletown, DE
25 February 2022

61796207R00126